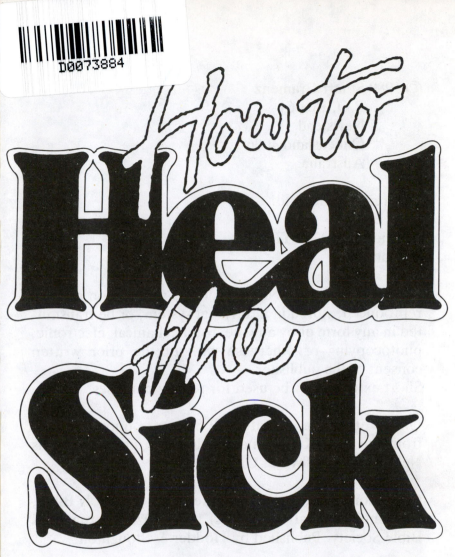

How to Heal the Sick

THROUGH THE POWER OF JESUS CHRIST

by
Stuart Gramenz

© 1989 Stuart Gramenz
P.O. Box 64
Newstead
Queensland 4006
Australia

Sovereign World Ltd.
P.O. Box 17
Chichester PO20 6YB
England

Unless otherwise indicated all Scripture quotations are from the New King James Bible copyright © Thomas Nelson Inc., Nashville, U.S.A.

Quotations marked NIV are taken from The Holy Bible, New International Version © 1973, 1978 International Bible Society. Published by Hodder & Stoughton.

Words of Scripture printed in heavy type are used by the writer for specific emphasis.

ISBN 1 85240 010 2

INDEX

Testimony of Dr. K. Ananada Rao
Neurology Section, St. Josephs
General Hospital, Guntur, India

I had the good fortune of attending all the meetings conducted by the 'JESUS HEALS' team in March 1983. Stuart Gramenz, the leader of the team, invited a number of deaf mute children aged about 9-10 years and also a leper onto the stage. After the sermon he took the children one by one and put his hands on them and prayed, praying that they could hear and speak.

To the pleasant surprise of thousands present the children were able to hear and speak, and repeat words like 'Mummy' and 'Daddy'. Later Brother Gramenz took the leper, put his hands on him and prayed; in a few moments the leper who had crippled hands and devoid of any sensation was able to stretch his fingers as well as have the feeling return to them.

As a doctor I would say these miracles are incomprehensible, as I know in deaf mutism the deafness was due to non development. The auditory nerve, internal ear, or the part of the brain where the auditory sensations are recognised are not developed.

In these cases all the children were deaf mutes unable to hear and never pronounced a single syllable in their life. Thank God — the Lord Jesus Christ made them whole.

In the case of the leper it takes years of treatment to have the disease halted. Certain symptoms will still remain like crippled and shortened fingers and thickened nerves.

But what was more, Brother Stuart jumped for joy, praising the name of the Lord, and hugged the leper with all the love and affection that only a parent could give. I wonder if my own mother would hug me like that if I were to be a leper.

I don't believe any doctor in the world is able to do these things, and I do not have any medical explanation for such happenings. Only God can do this in His Love for humanity.

DR. K. ANANADA RAO
M.B., M.S., C.S. (ENGLAND), F.R.C.S. (EDINBURGH)

INTRODUCTION

One of the greatest losses to the Church has been the ministry of prayer for the sick.

In recent times we have seen restoration of the principles of prayer, praise, and other important weapons of warfare. These have been taught and implemented in line with God's intention to restore all the former truths to the Church. Many truths on the subject of healing have been restored in recent years, yet the power to heal the sick still rests in the hands of what appears to be a divinely favoured "few", while the majority remain "armchair" spectators.

These spectators may be divided into two main groups: one, unaware of their ability, because they have never tried to heal the sick; the other, aware of their inability, because they have tried to heal the sick and failed.

But praying for the sick is not a matter of "having it", or "not having it". God has laid down basic principles that enable all believers to pray for the sick. These principles can be taught, learned and applied.

We have found that when key principles of healing have been imparted to Christians, a fresh new boldness has begun in their witness. A harvest of healing has come to previously barren areas.

The need for these principles to be imparted is obvious; for in sad contrast to the New Testament book of Acts, the Church as a whole is not ministering the apostolic doctrine of healing. The world waits for a Church which not only can teach, but demonstrate God's Kingdom benefits to mankind. Wholeness needs to be seen in the life of the believer, in keeping sickness from his own doorstep, before he or she can effectively reach out to help others.

The principles revealed in this book are not mere "head knowledge" or empty theories. They are based on Bible examples, and on the practice of those examples in praying for many thousands at home and on the mission field.

We trust that the book will inspire hope, faith and action in the Body of Christ, so this total Gospel of the Kingdom will be preached to every nation.

Stuart Gramenz

This book is an expansion of a previous book by the author called "How you can Heal the Sick" written in 1984. It was highly successful with three printings. After a further 5 years experience, many more truths have become evident to Stuart; he felt the need for this edition with all his latest teaching.

Chapter One

A CHALLENGE FOR THE MIRACULOUS

The need for a restoration of the truths of healing is so important today, for two major reasons. Firstly, when parents see their children sick, their love drives them to do all in their power to see them healed and well again.

Similarly, our heavenly Father wishes His children to be healed. Jesus only did the Father's will, and demonstrated His love by healing everybody who came to Him.

"Now Jesus went about . . . healing all kinds of sickness and all kinds of diseases among the people." (Matthew 4:23).

". . . And He cast out the spirits with a word, and healed all who were sick." (Matthew 8:16).

". . . And great multitudes followed Him, and He healed them all." (Matthew 12:15).

". . . Who went about doing good and healing all who were oppressed by the devil . . ." (Acts 10:38).

Healing demonstrates the Father heart of a God who still wishes to draw every person on this earth to Himself.

Secondly, Jesus used the healings as a sign and proof of His divinity.

When confronted with a crippled man in Luke 5, Jesus forgave him his sins. The religious men present were upset by this and queried His authority to forgive sin.

He challenged them and said:

"Which is easier, to say, 'Your sins are forgiven you,' or to say, 'Rise up and walk'?" (verse 23).

Now, of course, any person can say: "Your sins are forgiven you."

That's the deception in many religions in the world. Any priest in a cult can simply say: "Your sins are forgiven". Jesus goes on with His challenge:

"But that you may know that the Son of Man has power on earth to forgive sins."

He said to the man who was paralysed: *"I say to you, arise, take up your bed, and go to your house."*

The man was healed, but the event shook the people: " *... They were all amazed, and they glorified God ... "*

The miracle silenced His critics and proved beyond doubt His ability to forgive sin.

My Experience

During an evangelistic crusade in India in 1982, I was challenged in a new and exciting way.

We had been involved for a few years with large crusades with tens of thousands declaring their allegiance to Jesus. We were noticing, however, amid all this apparent success, a problem arising. The majority of our listeners were Hindu idol worshippers with millions of gods.

Many of these people, when making a decision for Jesus, were just accepting Him as another god and simply adding His name to the total. It is not uncommon in "Christian" homes to find a picture of Jesus on the wall and a picture of Krishna beside Him.

The problem was obvious - we had to get the people to renounce all the other gods and receive Jesus as their one and only Saviour.

However, the solution was not so apparent.

It was the final day of our crusade in Vishakhapatnam and I was waiting on the Lord as to what I should preach that night. The Lord led me to the story in 1 Kings 18:20-40, where Elijah faced a similar challenge at Mount Carmel.

The children of Israel had turned away from God and were worshipping the idol Baal. God instructed Elijah to challenge the prophets of Baal to a competition.

Both parties were to set up a bullock sacrifice. The prophets were to pray to their god to bring fire down from heaven and consume the sacrifice. Elijah was to do the same. Whichever answered the prayer and consumed the sacrifice would be proclaimed God.

When Elijah explained the challenge to the people they agreed it was a fair competition.

Elijah allowed the false prophets to pray first. All day they prayed, prophesied, shouted, jumped and even slashed themselves in an effort to move the hand of Baal. By evening nothing had happened.

Elijah had been mocking them throughout the whole time: *"Cry aloud, for he is a god; either he is meditating, or he is busy, or he is on a journey, or perhaps he is sleeping and must be awakened." (verse 27).* Adding to the prophets' humiliation, Elijah saturated his sacrifice with twelve pots of water.

He then declared: *"Hear me, O Lord, hear me, that this people may know that You are the Lord God, and that You have turned their hearts back to You again." (verse 37).*

Immediately, fire fell from heaven and consumed the sacrifice and the stones it rested on!

"Now when all the people saw it, they fell on their faces; and they said, 'The Lord, He is God! The Lord, He is God!' (verse 39).

Now It's Your Turn!

"What a wonderful message you have given to me Lord," I thought excitedly. "The people in India love stories and I know this will really bring the point clearly to them."

"That's not all," the Lord said to me. "You are going to have a contest as well! You are going to challenge the local religious leaders to a competition! After you preach, you will call the lepers, the deaf and the dumb onto the platform. If their religious leaders can heal them through their idols' power, let them be God, but if I heal them, Jesus is Lord."

I was really taken aback! It was an exciting concept, but the thought of actually doing it horrified me.

I thought of all the wonderful men whom God had used in the healing ministry, and how great it would have been for them to have had this opportunity.

The apostle Paul would have revelled in it. Smith Wigglesworth would have done a great job. T.L. Osborn would have been a huge success. The trouble was . . . they weren't there . . . and I was! I had no choice. It was of little benefit continuing the way we had, leaving people worshipping both Jesus and idols.

Thousands poured into the grounds that night and I stood up and preached the message of Elijah versus Baal.

The people loved the story. They laughed at the failure of the false prophets. They applauded the miracle of Elijah, little realising what was coming up next.

After I had finished, I said: "Your religious leaders tell you that YOUR gods forgive sin, but I'm telling you tonight that only Jesus can forgive sin.

"One of us tells the truth, the other lies.

"We are going to establish once and for all who is telling the truth. Tonight we are going to have a competition. We have the lepers, deaf, dumb and others here who need healing.

"Surely a God who has the almighty power to forgive our sins, can do something as simple as heal a person.

"I challenge the religious leaders to prove their gods' ability to forgive sin. Come up and heal the lepers; if they are healed we'll know your god is Lord. However, if my Jesus heals the leper, we'll know that He is Lord.

"Is that a fair competition?"

Everyone went completely silent.

"Is that a fair competition?" I repeated.

The people quietly nodded their heads. "Then come up here right now and represent your gods."

There was a stunned silence around the ground - nobody moved. I began to make a joke of them, just as Elijah did:

"What! Is there no one here to represent the local gods . . . nobody?

"At least the prophets of Baal made an attempt."

Still no one came.

I walked over to a leper, who had been in that condition for years, and said: "To show you that only One

11

is able to forgive sin and that He is Lord . . . be healed in the Name of Jesus Christ."

That same power that flowed into Elijah's sacrifice flowed into the leper. He started to rub his hands together excitedly. Feeling and movement had been restored. He raised his hands to the crowd, waving excitedly and showing them how his leprosy had been healed.

"You have to make a decision tonight," I said to the crowd, "It is either your gods or Jesus!"

In one accord the people stood to give their lives to Jesus and renounce the other gods.

I can assure you that throughout the whole ordeal, I was a frightened man, hanging tightly onto God. I could totally identify with Paul when he was in Corinth: *"I was with you in weakness, in fear, and in much trembling, and my speech and my preaching were not with persuasive words of human wisdom, but in demonstration of the Spirit and of power, that your faith should not be in the wisdom of men but in the power of God." (1 Corinthians 2:3-5).*

I found through experience that God does want to demonstrate His power mightily, and will work through those who are willing to believe what he says . . . and do it!

Same Today!

Once again today, God is wanting to bring a demonstration of His might and power so that Jesus may be glorified.

Some have said to me: "Stuart, there are some people who have been won to Christ without any signs and wonders!"

Yes, that's true. That's just the problem, it is only SOME PEOPLE.

Some did simply believe the words of Jesus, but there was another category who believed only after they saw the miracles.

To this group of people Jesus said: *"Even though you do not believe Me, believe the miracles, that you may know and understand that the Father is in Me and I am in the Father."* *(John 10:38 N.I.V.).*

It is very difficult for the majority of "natural" people to know and understand that Jesus can live in us. It does not make sense. However, when they SEE a miracle in the body, it helps them to receive the truth of the possibility of God living inside them.

Paul advocates this same thinking when he says: *". . . I will know, not the word of those who are puffed up, but the power. For the kingdom of God is not in word but in power."* *(1 Corinthians 4:19,20).*

All around the world there are many people who are disillusioned with the words of pompous, religious men. There needs to be shown the reality of God, not just in nice words but in power.

Heavy Spiritual Blindness

In Isaiah 60:2 it talks of a time when *"darkness shall cover the earth and gross darkness the people"*.

"Gross darkness" occurs when the people reject or have no spiritual knowledge of the Living God.

I believe the majority of people in the world are in this position today. "Gross darkness" is in every nation, with people worshipping false gods, man's ability, man's philosophies or even *"having a form of godliness but denying its power . . . " (2 Timothy 3:5).*

There are great orators and writers who are enticing people away from a relationship with Jesus with clever words and speech.

What did Paul say again?

"And my speech and my preaching were not with persuasive words of human wisdom, but in demonstration of the Spirit and of power, that your faith should not be in the wisdom of men but in the power of God." (1 Corinthians 2:4-5).

Gross darkness existed in the days of Jesus and Paul. If they needed signs and wonders to achieve a clear understanding of the kingdom of God, surely we need to operate in power to achieve similar results.

It takes more than words in many cases to smash through the gross blindness that surrounds them. "Gross darkness" is flooding through the earth and at the same time God is raising up and restoring a people who will once again be able to duplicate the ministries of the early church.

". . . When the enemy comes in like a flood, the Spirit of the Lord will lift up a standard against him." (Isaiah 59:19).

We are His standard in the earth today. He is training and restoring former truths so that we will rise up and flood the world with truth and confirm it with the power of God.

What About False Healings?

Many reports have come in to us about healings that are not done in the name of Jesus. Although these seem to be sparse and many times unconfirmed, we must realise that the devil does have some power and will use even healing if it means he can hold onto people. It is a small price to pay to ensure he has them in hell.

However, these "healings" have been used in some places as an excuse not to pray for the sick.

Surely we must realize that the devil is a counterfeiter, a copier of anything Jesus does. He wants people to worship him and will do anything he can to get that praise.

He also counterfeits righteousness, and many cults teach that they are the way to achieve holiness.

Do we also stop preaching righteousness through Christ because of their teachings? Remember, Church, we are the standard and are commanded to teach, preach and heal. The devil can never maintain the high standard that Christ performs!

Moses' Example

I've had concerned pastors come to me when we challenge the cults, communists and others to prove their gods and philosophies by healing lepers or other so-called "incurable" illness.

"What if some religious man or witch doctor gets up and performs a miracle?" I have been asked on many occasions.

What happened in the court of Pharaoh when God was demonstrating His power through Moses? Aaron threw down his rod and it turned into a snake after a command from Moses. Pharaoh summoned his court magicians and they then duplicated the miracle.

That probably would have shaken the faith of most people today. They may have run out of the court. However Moses, a humble man who trusted in His God, didn't move and watched the greater miracle. Aaron's rod ate all the sorcerers' rods!

Today our God is still able to do the bigger miracle. His standard of power and righteousness is unparalleled.

Do you believe that?

Then if we believe it, we should preach it and demonstrate it without any fear or concern. We have a God whose hand is not shortened and who still has the power to deliver. He wants to demonstrate His standard to the world.

He needs standard bearers, with the spirit of Elijah and Moses who will dare to believe once again that He is the great "I AM".

Not up to standard?

"We are not at that level yet," you may be thinking.

Before an army goes to war, it goes through training where the use of all basic weapons is taught. Soldiers learn to shoot their rifles and throw their grenades. The basic weaponry of the Church is preaching, healing and casting out demons. At present, we are in a "boot camp", learning how to use these weapons to their fullest. Reading this "army manual" and applying its principles will help raise you to the standard of the soldier that God requires.

We are not expecting that after reading this book you will go out and see everybody healed.

Healing is like a rifle. It is a weapon that you will learn

how to handle and then practise with. Once you have learned the principles, you now will perhaps see two or three healed out of ten, instead of, say, one out of fifty previously. As, you practice using the information in this book, your results should continue to increase.

Gollapalli Narayana Swamy, from the town of Peddapurappadu, a Hindu, was a leper for 10 years. In 1980 we prayed for him and he was healed. Since accepting the Lord that time he has preached the Gospel and witnessed how Jesus heals and saves.

Chapter 2

CAN ALL CHRISTIANS HEAL THE SICK?

As a young Christian I excitedly read of the wonderful healings and miracles which Jesus did. I expected that God wanted to, and would heal people the same today.

After all, Jesus Christ is the same yesterday, today and forever (Hebrews 13:8). My mistake however, was to think that He would only use the priest, pastor or the evangelist for this task, while I was to take on the role of an excited spectator.

One day back in 1979, a Scripture that I had read many times before suddenly leapt out at me. A Scripture that was to ultimately change my direction and give me the extra joy and excitement that had been missing from my Christian experience.

Jesus said in John 14:12:

"Most assuredly, I say to you, he who believes in Me, the works that I do he will do also; and greater works than these he will do, because I go to My Father."

What Are 'The Works'?

Acts 10:38 tells us: *"How God anointed Jesus of Nazareth with the Holy Spirit and with power, who went about doing good and healing all who were oppressed by the devil, for God was with Him."*

Two areas of works are given here:
1. Doing good;
2. Healing all.

Firstly, we are expected to exhibit a Godly character doing good works. This is an area which has received the majority of instruction in the Church at large. Most of us are very much aware of our role in this area of helping mankind. We feed the hungry, provide for the poor, look after widows and orphans, and the like.

However, the second part is just as important, if we wish to be obedient to all of the Scriptures. By "healing all that are oppressed of the devil" we certainly would be helping mankind in another form.

Notice the emphasis that Jesus uses in John 14:12: *"The works that I do will you do also."*

Just as we are to exhibit Godly character and to do good works, we are to heal. This was not an optional extra, it was a command. That knowledge really released me. Not only was I supposed to heal the sick, but I was EXPECTED to do it.

His Disciples Only

For years, I was under the impression that Jesus was only talking to Peter, John and the other disciples. I thought it must have been so great and exciting to live back in those days.

But the revelation of John 14:12 impacted on me: *"HE THAT BELIEVES ON ME"* will do my works!

Jesus was not only talking to His immediate disciples, but to me and every other believer!

I noted most importantly, that it did not say a group of

Christians together with collective works, would do the works. It meant the individual, he or she who believed on Him could do these works.

Other translations of the Scripture only confirmed my excitement:

"I assure you that the man who believes in Me will do the same things that I have done . . . " (J.B. Phillips).

"In most solemn truth I tell you that he who trusts in Me . . . the things which I do he shall do also . . . " (Weymouth).

"I tell you the truth, anyone who has faith in Me will do what I have been doing." (N.I.V.)

Truthfully, most definitely, most assuredly anyone who has faith in Jesus has an opportunity to pray for and to see the sick healed!

The realisation of this promise was the beginning of a new life for me with the opportunity of praying for, and seeing, thousands and thousands healed.

Since that time, our organisation has taken over 1,500 everyday Christians on our crusades into India and other Third World countries. They have not been full time missionaries, just ones with a heart to reach the lost and see the power of God work through them.

The majority knew very little about power ministry when they came. On these training trips, we teach them how to preach, how to heal and cast out demons and then release them on the streets during the day and the crusade crowds at night. Everyone has seen results in the miraculous.

After this training and experience, they return to their hometown to continue the ministry.

We are now training other evangelists and pastors in

the Jesus-style ministry, so that this can be multiplied even further.

Many Christians have missed out on one of the greatest blessings that Jesus wants us to participate in. My prayer is that as you will read on, and allow principles and keys in this book to sink into your heart, you will never be the same again.

Can WE heal?

Many Christians have had difficulty with the fact of our doing the healing.

The confusion comes because, in some Scriptures, the healing is attributed to the particular person.

Paul prays for fever: *"And it happened that the father of Publius lay sick of a fever and dysentery. Paul went in to him and prayed, and he laid his hands on him AND HEALED HIM."* (Acts 28:8).

Philip in Samaria: *"And the multitudes with one accord heeded the things spoken by Philip, hearing and seeing the miracles WHICH HE DID."* (Acts 8:6).

Both Scriptures give Philip and Paul the credit. However in Acts 3:12 we find that Peter, after raising a cripple, gave the explanation: *"Men of Israel, why do you marvel at this? Or why look so intently at us, as though by our own power or godliness we had made this man walk?"* Peter healed him, but not through HIS power.

When you feel sick and go to a doctor, he prescribes you medicine. You take the medicine and are healed.

Did the doctor heal you? He was used as a way to dispense the medicine to you. Similarly God uses us as dispensers of His healing power.

Our aim will be to teach you how to prescribe and administer God's healing power.

God's Recipe for Healing

There are many who misunderstand God's divine healing principles. If Jesus told us we SHALL do His works, He must have made a way possible for us to achieve it. Otherwise, the Scripture in John 14:12 is false. Many have thought that in healing, you either had an ability to heal or you didn't. You either have "it" or don't have "it".

When Jesus taught, He often used parables. These explain spiritual truths in clear and simple terms.

Divine healing has been a truth that many have had difficulty grasping, so we are giving modern parables to help alleviate the problem.

Most of us understand the principles of cooking. If you are going to bake a good cake, first of all you need a recipe.

The recipe has a list of ingredients and procedures; when followed exactly, it results in success.

God has spiritual "recipes" for healing in His Word. When they are adhered to, they will produce healings. Obviously, when baking a cake, if ingredients are omitted or procedures are not followed, the result is a flop.

There have been many "flops" among Christians in divine healing, not because they didn't have the ability, but through lack of knowledge of God's recipes and the ingredients. In this book we are going to cover some of God's recipes for healing and clearly define the ingredients.

First Recipe

Our first "recipe" for healing is found in Mark 16:15-18: *"Go into all the world and preach the Gospel to every creature. And these signs will follow those who believe: in My name they will cast out demons; . . . they will lay hands on the sick, and they will recover."*

Here, we have step-by-step directions for divine healing. A spiritual recipe with three basic ingredients. Once understood and followed, we have a promise that "these signs shall follow those who believe".

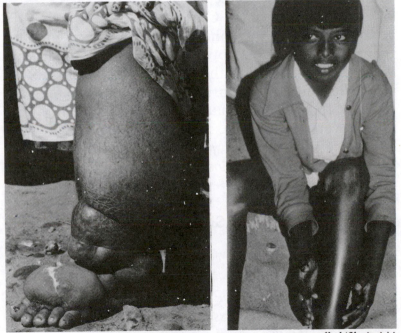

Elephantiasis results from a mosquito bite. A microscopic worm called 'filariasis' is transferred from the mosquito. This boy shows where the size of his leg was previously. After prayer his leg shrunk instantly.

Chapter 3

A GOSPEL OF POWER

Our first ingredient in Mark 16:15,17 & 18 says:
"Go and preach the Gospel."
Notice the order in which Jesus' recipe for healing is given.

It does not say: "Go and heal the sick." It says: "Preach the Gospel."

That is our first step. If you were baking a cake and you got your procedures and ingredients out of order, you wouldn't have much success.

Yet, this is how many Christians can mess up God's recipe. They hear someone is sick, and go and pray for them. In most cases, it flops, and then they wonder what went wrong. They read the recipe back to front.

The disciples, after hearing the instruction for healing in Mark 16:15-17, went out and did exactly as they were told. In verse 20 it tells us:
"And they went out and preached everywhere, the Lord working with them and confirming the word through the accompanying signs."
What did they do first? They preached the Gospel!

What then happened? Signs and wonders followed the preaching!

Look how Jesus did it:
"Now Jesus went about all Galilee, teaching in their synagogues, preaching the Gospel of the kingdom, and healing all kinds of sickness and all kinds of disease among the people." (Matthew 4:23).

He preached the Gospel, and then He healed.

Why Doesn't It Work For Me?

A second problem can now arise, as we attempt to grasp this initial truth.

Many have questioned this teaching, based on either their own or other people's experience.

"I've preached the Gospel and no signs and wonders followed me," one might say.

Do we believe your experience, or what the Bible teaches?

"But I know a well known evangelist and he preaches the Gospel and no signs and wonders follow him!" another one would say.

Do we believe man's experiences, or what the Bible teaches?

When the Bible says if we preach the Gospel and signs and wonders shall follow, and yet some are preaching with no signs and wonders following, perhaps we had better look at what is being preached.

Now, I am not trying to suggest that some people are preaching another Gospel, or a wrong message. But I believe in many cases, that the Gospel is preached in part, and not in the fullness that Jesus and His disciples preached it.

Partial Gospel means partial results, and this is why we do not see the signs and wonders.

For instance if you are going to learn to swim there are two basic components needed for success ... the arm action and the kick.

If I throw you into the pool and you have perfect arm action and yet you still sink; you would quickly realise that something is wrong with the kick.

In preaching the Gospel, many of us are getting part of it, the arm action, right.

What is the arm action?

We have been preaching the portion of the Gospel which says basically: "If you receive Jesus Christ as Lord, you will have eternal life."

Is it the truth?

Of course it is. It is the very heart of the Gospel message. It is of little benefit to be healed and not saved. However this is not the entire Gospel.

We may have had perfect arm action in preaching eternal life, but when it comes to signs and wonders, we sink.

What do we need to do? We need to put the "kick" back in the Gospel.

We have to preach the power kick which produces healings.

What Is Lacking?

Gospel, of course, means "good news". When Jesus preached, he preached more than the good news of eternal life.

Let us look at Luke 4:18 where Jesus reads prophecy about Himself from the book of Isaiah. Here are incorporated many of the promises of the message He has for mankind. He first of all says:

"The Spirit of the Lord is upon Me, Because He has anointed Me to preach the Gospel to the poor."

He then lists the benefits and blessings:

1. "HE HAS SENT ME TO HEAL THE BROKEN-HEARTED."

Obviously, there are many people in the world who have been hurt emotionally, children from broken homes, and others of us who have been wounded through relationships and contacts with other people. For those with emotional hurts and rejection, Jesus says "I have good news, you can be healed."

2. "TO PREACH DELIVERANCE TO THE CAPTIVES."

Every person in the world has been blinded by the devil. They are in captivity to him and they need release. The good news says you can be delivered, set free, born again, by repenting and accepting Jesus as your Lord.

3. "RECOVERY OF SIGHT TO THE BLIND."

This speaks of the physical afflictions which beset so many people. The good news is that Jesus heals all. You can be set free from leprosy, polio, or whatever sickness or disease you have.

4. "TO SET AT LIBERTY THOSE WHO ARE OPPRESSED."

Jesus went around healing all who were oppressed of the devil. All those with spiritual oppression or possession could be set free.

5. "TO PREACH THE ACCEPTABLE YEAR OF THE LORD."

The acceptable year of the Lord was the year of Jubilee where anyone in any form of captivity or slavery or bondage was released. Jesus says if any sin or sickness has you in slavery or bondage, you don't have to wait any longer. You can be healed today.

". . . Today this Scripture is fulfilled in your hearing." (verse 21).

He preached that mankind could be set free - spirit, soul and body - from any affliction.

Those who heard the words which Jesus spoke, believed them and reached out to Him they were set free of whatever bondage they had.

"Jesus, heal my hurts," one would say.

"Jesus, forgive my sins," another would plead.

"Jesus, heal my body," others would cry out.

All those who believed and reached out in faith were released.

"He healed them all." (Matthew 8:16, 12:15, Luke 6:19)

Now Jesus instructed His disciples to go and preach this same Gospel - they did and repeated His works.

Is this the Gospel you have been preaching to others? Have you given them ALL the promises that God has for them? Or have you, like many others, only been preaching one aspect . . . that of eternal life?

Understand that if you only preach eternal life, all they can have faith for is eternal life. However, if we preach as Jesus preached, offering eternal life and healing of soul and body as well, they can receive faith for all aspects, and not only be born again but healed as well. Faith comes by hearing the Word, but if we don't hear the Word of healing, then no faith can rise for it.

It is such a simple truth, but it is often the simple things we fail to do.

Mixing Faith

Hebrews 4:2 says: *"For indeed the Gospel was preached to us as well as to them; but the word which they heard did not profit them, not being mixed with faith in those who heard it."*

28

In other words, those who were healed heard the good news as well as all the others, for . . .

ALL HEARD THE MESSAGE . . .

"BUT the word preached did not profit them, not being mixed with faith in them that heard it."

Every person got to hear the message of Christ, yet, unless they mixed it with faith and said: "yes, I believe it and accepted it," they did not receive the benefits of it.

In the future let us ensure that we preach the whole message, that Christ came to destroy sin, sickness and any other aspect of the devil's work. Faith can then rise up in their hearts. If they reach out for the answer in Christ, they can be set free from whatever is binding them.

How To Raise A Cripple

This faith ingredient is clearly demonstrated in a story in Acts 14, as it shows us how to raise a cripple. I'm sure we would all like to be used to heal this kind of person. It is exciting, and we have seen this happen in our ministry many times.

"And in Lystra a certain man without strength in his feet was sitting, a cripple from his mother's womb, who had never walked. This man heard Paul speaking. Paul, observing him intently and seeing that he had faith to be healed, said with a loud voice: 'Stand up straight on your feet!' And he leapt and walked." (verses 8, 9, 10)

You may be thinking now: "Oh well, if I must have the faith that Paul had, then I'll never raise anybody. After all, he was a miracle worker, an especially anointed man."

We wrongly assume in this case that it was Paul's faith

that raised the cripple.

Look carefully at what it says in verse 9:

"Paul observing him intently and seeing that he had faith to be healed." Who had the faith to be healed ?

THE CRIPPLE HAD THE FAITH!

Now doesn't that make it very simple? All we need to do is to find cripples who have the faith to be healed and command them to stand.

Can you picture yourself just going down hospital wards, to those who have faith to be healed that are in wheel chairs. Like Paul you simply walk up to them and say: "Arise, stand up straight on your feet." So many problems could be solved if they had the faith.

Faith Is the Answer

There now arises a new challenge.

HOW DO YOU GET FAITH INTO THE PEOPLE?

How did this man, who has been crippled since birth, suddenly get the empowering faith to be healed?

To get the answer, we must read the entire story. I intentionally omitted the key ingredient. We need to go back to the verse just prior to this healing miracle where it tells us: *"And they were preaching the Gospel there." (verse 7).*

What happened as a result of the preaching? The man heard the Gospel and suddenly he had faith for his healing.

What do you think Paul preached to him? Do you think all that Paul gave him was a message based on: "If you believe in Jesus Christ, you shall have eternal life"?

Do you really think after hearing only that, he would

say "My goodness, I've got faith for my crippled legs to be healed"?

Of course he wouldn't.

Paul's Good News

I believe this would have been the kind of message Paul preached.

I can picture him, probably with lepers, the blind, alongside that cripple. Paul would have stood up and preached the good news found in Luke 4:18. He added that now, through the sacrifice of Jesus Christ at Calvary, these blessings were obtainable.

I can see him preaching:

"Christ crucified, His blood shed on Calvary means we no longer have to bear the burden of sin. Man can be set free by simply accepting that sacrifice. He had His back whipped and has borne all sickness and disease upon His body so that mankind can be healed.

"Isaiah 53:4 & 5: 'Surely He has borne our griefs and carried our sorrows; yet we esteemed Him stricken, smitten by God, and afflicted. But He was wounded for our transgressions, He was bruised for our iniquities; the chastisement for our peace was upon Him and by His stripes we are healed.'

"By accepting this sacrifice, men and women, your sins can be forgiven, the lepers can be cleansed, the blind can see, the crippled can walk!"

What happened to the cripple? The man heard Paul speaking. Paul, observing him intently, and seeing that he had faith to be healed, said with a loud voice: "Stand up straight on your feet," and he leapt and he walked.

Now it may be a little clearer to you why some

evangelists and perhaps you yourself are not getting healing results along with seeing people born again. If you are not preaching healing and believing for it, results will be hard to find.

Believe As Little Children

Many of us have great difficulty grasping the whole truth ourselves, much less preaching it, but God is restoring His word to us. We need to be like little children. First we accept it, and then we preach it, expecting results.

Because of our backgrounds in Christianity, one day we were born again, next month water baptized, perhaps months later filled with the Holy Ghost, and then we received an occasional healing. As as a result of this, we can find ourselves expecting little more for those to whom we are preaching.

I remember how the Lord released my faith in this area. I was reading the Scriptures we had just quoted in Isaiah 53, and also 1 Peter 2:24, which says:

"Who Himself bore our sins in His own body on the tree, that we, having died to sins, might live for righteousness - by whose stripes you were healed."

Suddenly I realised something I hadn't seen before. I said: "Lord, if you bore both sin and sickness on the cross, then when people come to the cross, they should be able to have both sin and sickness removed at the same time."

"Yes!" the Lord said.

Now this shocked me, because in my early ministry I would only get people saved and then perhaps later in the meeting, pray for sickness.

The Lord told me if I preached the entire message, I would see salvation of spirit, soul and body at the same time. I decided that is what I would do on my next overseas crusade.

The first night at the crusade I preached on Isaiah 53 and 1 Peter 2:24 and the message of restoration. "Jesus Christ died on that cross at Calvary," I told them. "He bore both sin and sickness".

"After three days He rose from the dead and told His disciples to go into all the world and tell every person what He did for us.

"I am one of Jesus's disciples tonight," I continued, "Jesus has sent me here to tell you this good news. If you believe my words tonight you can have your sin forgiven and be set free from your sicknesses."

Firstly, I asked for those who believed that Jesus Christ had died for their sin. Hands went up everywhere, and they followed my prayer, accepting Jesus Christ as their Lord.

I then asked who among them believed that Jesus Christ bore their sickness. Again their hands went up. Together we confessed faith in the word, and they confessed they believed they had received their healing. "Act your faith," I called out, "Move about; you'll find that pains have left your body; sickness is gone !" The crowd began to get to their feet and move about.

I looked to one side and saw a mother lifting her polio-stricken child. Limp sticks for legs were dangling from the little body, and the mother was feverishly trying to get him to walk. The little legs collapsed lifelessly. I looked away and said quietly to myself: "Lord have I missed it? Have I gone too far ?" Moments later I looked back, and the same child was walking by itself! The mother was jubilant and shouting! I tell you, there was only one person more excited than the mother ... that was the preacher!

I had believed that God's Word worked, but from that moment I "knew" that it worked. These people were able to accept the word, as simply "as little children", and the Kingdom of God came to them.

We who are preaching or praying can restrict God by our unbelief. After that incident, I have believed all and seen many great miracles of healing follow the preaching of the word.

"But That's Over There!"

On returning to Australia I preached to a small congregation and related the many miracles that had happened overseas. One could almost read their thoughts: "Oh but that's over there; God always seems to move more among the needy!"

I challenged them that they could have the same results here, if they simply believed the Word. God is the same everywhere. The only thing that changes is our belief. I then told them I would preach exactly the same message, and that those who received the word in simple faith would be healed.

The preaching was nearing an end when suddenly I saw shafts of light dropping on people as they listened. Faith had arisen and their faith was drawing the healing presence of God onto them. I became excited, stopped preaching, and asked for those who had been healed to get up and testify. All throughout the church people stood immediately and gave praise to the Lord. They had received it! The Scripture was fulfilled in their lives even before I had finished preaching!

Since that time I have seen the glory of the Lord many times in the form of light come into meetings and touch people as faith is raised. Think of the time we would save in healing lines if we could receive like that!

What a wonderful weapon of healing we have in our mouths!

Do you want to speak with more power?
Do you want to have a bold witness in your life?
Then pray this prayer aloud right now!

"Jesus Christ come into my life and make my spirit alive. I believe you died for my sins and rose again from the dead. Forgive me of my sins, help me turn from them and break every bondage in my life. Fill me with the power of the Holy Spirit to enable me to do your will. Amen."

John 3:1-9
Romans 10:9 & 10

Chapter 4

YOUR ACTIVE ENERGIZING WORD

Romans 1:16 tells us: *"For I am not ashamed of the Gospel of Christ, for it is the power of God to salvation . . . "* (spirit, soul and body) *to everyone who believes."*

What is the power?

THE GOSPEL IS THE POWER!

THE GOSPEL IS THE POWER!

If I said to you electricity is a power, you understand that. It contains an energy to perform a task.

The laser beam is a power. It is a force to achieve results.

The Gospel is THE power! It has the energy and force to achieve healing and salvation for people. This is important for you to understand because many have had a feeling of inadequacy when it comes to sharing Christ with others.

Does it say your eloquence and fluency of speech are the power?

Does it say your great oratory and strong voice are the power?

Does it say your good looks and great stature are the power?

THE GOSPEL IS THE POWER!

The message you preach has the power in it.

This is confirmed in Hebrews 4:12: *"For the word of God is living and powerful, and sharper than any two-edged sword. . ."*

Can you imagine a soldier, with a sad looking face, saying he hasn't got the looks or the voice to use his sword?

It doesn't matter if you are big or small, male or female, loud voiced or soft voiced, if you thrust a sword into somebody it has an effect.

We must learn to separate ourselves from the power. We are not the power. It is a weapon that is released every time we speak God's word.

Look at what the Amplified Bible says of Hebrews 4:12:

"God's word is alive and full of power - making it active, operative, energizing and effective."

When you speak God's word that power goes into men's hearts with an active energizing force that gives men an ability to believe the Gospel.

Because of that effective operative word, something inside says: "Yes, I need that, I need my sins forgiven, I need my body healed and I believe Jesus can do it."

John's Release

The reality of this helped me to be able to release many more people into this kind of ministry. People whom you perhaps would have initially thought had no ability to see others saved and healed.

This story happened in India quite some years ago to a man who, for his own protection, we will call "John".

In the natural John was a person who had difficulty in putting two words together. He was always stumbling in his speech and was devoid of any real confidence.

I would go out preaching in the Indian streets and he

would always come out with me. A more faithful man would be hard to find.

After I had preached solidly, morning and afternoon for a week, my throat was absolutely red raw. Stupidly, I kept preaching until I completely lost my voice. You do things like that when you are young and full of too much enthusiasm. One thing I have learnt is that you must give your body the rest it needs.

I was standing at the front door of the place where we were staying in a town called Kakinada just watching people passing the front door.

Next thing, a couple of Indian men walked up to me and began staring at me, looking me up and down. I was a white person and I guessed they hadn't seen too many. Initially this was a little embarrassing, but I decided to imitate them and look them up and down as well. They thought that was hilarious and began to laugh.

This soon attracted the attention of others.

Soon we had four, then ten and finally about twenty five to thirty men, all standing and looking me up and down and I was returning the compliment. Everyone was enjoying the joke.

Suddenly I realised that I had a potential Church standing in front of me. I tried to preach and only a squeak came out. At that moment John came down the steps and stood beside me, wondering what all the commotion was.

I whispered to him: "John, preach to these people".

I have never seen a person go the colours that John did at that moment. He was initially speechless and then blurted out: "You know I'll do anything for you. But don't ask me to preach. I'm hopeless."

I said to Him: "If you don't preach, these men will probably go to hell."

That sobered him up, and as terrified as he was, he began to speak to them.

We've taken about 1500 people into third world countries and trained them and I've heard some bad preaching. However, none was as bad as John's. When people are nervous they say the first thing that comes into their mind. He gave almost a Sunday School message with the story of the baby Jesus in the manger, visits by the shepherds and wise men and all the trivialities you could imagine.

I kept nudging him:, "The Gospel, the Gospel!"

"Yes," he said nervously. "I'm getting there."

He preached all over the place, with constant interruptions of "ums" and "ers". It was absolutely so bad, I was just hoping that no Christians were listening.

Eventually he got around to the cross and Christ's sacrifice and finally asked for those who wanted to receive Jesus as Lord.

To my utter amazement, hands went up everywhere. I was absolutely stunned and I said: "Well Lord, that proves it for me. THE GOSPEL HAS TO BE THE POWER TO SALVATION. IT CERTAINLY HAD NOTHING TO DO WITH JOHN."

The early disciples weren't great orators. Some were uneducated fishermen. Paul said:

"And I, brethren, when I came to you, did not come with excellence of speech or of wisdom declaring to you the

testimony of God. For I determined not to know anything among you except Jesus Christ and Him crucified."

"And my speech and my preaching were not with persuasive words of human wisdom, but in demonstration of the Spirit and of power, that your faith should not be in the wisdom of men but in the power of God." (1 Corinthians 2:1,2,4,5).

God doesn't need orators and intellectual speakers. He wants people who will unashamedly preach Christ's crucifixion and the benefits of it. If we preach it as Paul did, we will see the powerful signs and wonders confirming the word. Like Paul said, it will demonstrate that people should have no faith in man's wisdom, but only in the power of God.

Overcoming Fear

In that passage, using only verses 1, 2, 4 and 5, we can get the impression that Paul was fearless and bold. I purposely left verse 3 out of that section so we could study it separately. In the midst of all these confident statements he says in verse 3:

"I was with you in weakness, in fear, and in much trembling."

Isn't that how many of us feel when we think of having to preach? Yet Paul didn't take any notice of that. He knew he had a weapon that, once released, would win the day.

We need to be very aware of this weapon we have in our mouths.

You may face "weakness and much trembling" yourself, but placing confidence in your weapons and not in yourself will help remove fear.

Sharpening the Sword

Like any good soldier, you need to practise before going onto the battlefield. Read the chapter on the Gospel again and again. Get other books on it, so that you know all aspects of your weapon. Then you will be able to put up a great fight on the field.

Keep It Simple

One thing you really need to remember, is to keep your preaching simple. People can look at a well known evangelist or speaker and think they need to copy his preaching style.

Most importantly, be yourself and give out the good news in a free and easy manner. Use examples of what Jesus has done for you or others you know of personally.

Basically, the disciples were only giving their personal testimonies of how Jesus changed them and others they knew about.

Giving personal stories gives the Gospel life and reality and will help touch the hearts of the listeners. Read Luke 4:18 again and see how simply Jesus preached.

Seed for a Need

When Christ preached his full Gospel message, He was preaching to a group among whom there were many needs. When speaking to an individual it is important for you to give the person a complete picture of this new

Kingdom, because Christ does fill every need. However, each person will have individual problems and it is wise to discuss these, and how Christ can fill those particular needs.

It would be of little use preaching to a rich old lady in a wheel chair about abundant finances. If you are preaching to village people who are experiencing drought, then Jesus can bring rain. If a marriage is on the rocks, then Jesus can restore it. What a wonderful new Kingdom we have entered into!

God's word, we are told, is like a seed. Plant it in somebody's heart and it will grow. Seed for a need!

While on an overseas flight, an air hostess approached me and offered some small prawn savouries. I took one and thanked her, but she just stood watching me. Then the most extraordinary thing happened. "Are you going to eat that?" she enquired. I was taken aback and replied: "Well I was going to." As I lifted it up, she said again: "Are you going to eat that?"

I couldn't believe it! I asked her if people got sick when they ate them. "Sometimes," she said.

That just does not happen on an international flight, so I felt that God was prompting me into action.

I told her that I had a God who protected me, then ate the savoury and promptly asked for two more. There were plenty of savouries, as she had obviously done a great job of slowing down the demand!

This request intrigued her. She brought back the savouries as I had asked, and watched as I ate them. As there were relatively few on the flight she kept returning to me, and telling me many more things about herself.

She had a problem, and was planning to return home to Bombay in a month. Her problem, believe it or not, was air sickness! I told her of our crusades in India and how Jesus had cleansed the lepers and raised the cripples.

What was I doing?

I was preaching the Gospel to her!

I told her that Jesus could meet her need, and if she would like prayer, I would pray for her. She agreed.

Praying for an air hostess's stomach in the aisle of a plane can be a little tricky. We managed to do it, with only about 80% of the passengers noticing!

At the end of the trip she came back to me elated, saying: "I haven't had any upsets at all." "Neither have I," I said, patting my prawn-filled stomach. "Who healed you?" I asked "Jesus," she replied. Now she was very open to hear more of the message.

I went and sat with her in the rear seat and told her the rest of the good news. She accepted the Lord just as we landed!

Chapter 5

"ELECTRIC" HANDS

After completing our initial ingredient of preaching the Gospel, we now go on to our next additive, the laying on of hands.

"These signs will follow those who believe ... they will lay hands on the sick and they will recover." (Mark 16:17-18).

This is not some new method for the Church. Hebrews 6:1-2 tells us that it is a basic doctrine, and that it was used through both Old and New Testaments for the transference of various things.

Sin

*"And Aaron shall **lay both his hands** on the head of the live goat, confess over it all the iniquities of the children of Israel, and all their transgressions, concerning all their sins, putting them on the head of the goat ... The goat shall bear on itself all their iniquities to an uninhabited land; and he shall release the goat into the wilderness." (Leviticus 16:21, 22).*

Sin was transferred onto the goat.

Wisdom

*"For Joshua the son of Nun was **full of the Spirit of Wisdom;** for Moses had **laid hands** upon him. (Deuteronomy 34:9).*
Wisdom was transferred to Joshua.

In these cases and many other examples, the laying on of hands represented transference from one to another.

Jesus' Ministry

Jesus also used this principle in healing. It was by placing His hands upon people or touching them. A woman was bent over with a bad back for eighteen years:

"But when Jesus saw her, He called her to Him and said to her, 'Woman, you are loosed from your infirmity.' And He LAID HIS HANDS ON HER, and immediately she was made straight, and glorified God." (Luke 13:12, 13).

He healed a leper in a similar manner:

"Then a leper came to Him, imploring Him, kneeling down to Him and saying to Him, 'If You are willing, You can make me clean.' And Jesus, moved with compassion, put out His hand and TOUCHED HIM and said to him 'I am willing; be cleansed." (Mark 1:40, 41).

Notice it is not some formal ceremony - by either laying hands or simply touching somebody, they were healed.

Disciples' Ministry

Again, we see that by the laying on of the hands of the disciples, healings took place: *"And it happened that the father of Publius lay sick of a fever and dysentery. Paul went in to him and prayed, and he laid his hands on him and healed him." (Acts 28:8).*

"And through the hands of the apostles many signs and wonders were done among the people." (Acts 5:12).

As we can see, the principle of laying on of hands was used by Jesus, and by His immediate disciples. And it is also able to be exercised by "those who believe". This means any "believer" can lay hands on the sick, and they

WILL recover!

How Did It Work?

We have found as people understand how divine healing operates, a new faith rises within them. Let's look at Jesus' ministry so you will actually know what happens when you begin to pray for people.

Jesus actually performed no healing ministry until, at the age of 30, He was filled with the Holy Spirit. In other words, all healing occurred as a result of the power of the Holy Spirit in Him.

To make this truth easier to grasp, we will make use of another modern day parable.

Most of us are aware of the operation of a car battery. You can remove the battery from an automobile and take it anywhere. It is portable power. If you put leads on your car battery and connect those leads to a conductor, such as a 12 volt light, the electricity will flow along the leads and into the conductor.

The Holy Spirit went into Jesus like a huge powerful portable battery. Whenever Jesus put His leads (His hands) onto a conductor (the person), the healing power in His "battery" would flow through His "leads" and into the person. In doing so, healing would take place. Like the sin being transferred by Aaron, and wisdom being transferred by Moses, Jesus transferred this healing power to others.

Luke 6:19 demonstrates this point very clearly:

"And the whole multitude sought to touch Him, for power went out from Him and healed them all."

Power came out!

What power?

The portable, Holy-Spirit-battery power!

"Alive" with Power

This power flowed whenever He touched somebody or somebody touched Him.

Have you ever touched an electrical appliance that was "alive"? You will receive an electric current through you.

It was the same if you were a conductor and you touched Jesus.

This is what happened to the woman with the issue of blood. She touched Him and the power flowed out of Him and into her. This is what Jesus tells us in Luke 8:46: *"Somebody touched Me, for I perceived power going out from Me."*

Notice we keep using the word "conductor". You need to be able to "conduct" the healing power of God. You become a conductor by faith. Jesus said of the woman in verse 48: *"Your faith has made you well. Go in peace."*

The principle of Mark 16 operates on a person's faith being raised, and then that person can conduct God's healing power.

However, faith is needed by both parties. Firstly, you the person praying must allow the healing power to flow through you, just as it did with Jesus.

Secondly, the person for whom you are praying, needs to be able to conduct the healing power just like the woman.

The faith required in both cases is different. Let's see first how much faith is required by you, and then how much is needed by the other person.

Your Faith

What does the Bible say about you?

"But you shall receive power when the Holy Spirit has come upon you . . . " (Acts 1:8).

Jesus was talking about the future: "You SHALL receive power."

Christians today, if we have asked the Holy Spirit to fill us, no longer have to say: "We shall receive power!" We can say: "WE HAVE RECEIVED POWER!"

The battery pack of the Holy Spirit is in YOU right now!

Many Spirit-filled believers seem to have trouble with that. After confessing they believe the promise of Acts 1:8, they then turn around and ask God for more.

"Lord, give me more power!"

"If I only had more, then I could do Your works!"

It's no use praying that prayer, if you are already filled with the Holy Spirit. You have all the power necessary to do the work.

What you have to do is to learn to have faith in what you've already received.

You have to settle it in your heart that the battery pack of power is in you right now. That way, your mind can catch up with the reality of what has happened to you.

Healing Trees

Let's help you renew your mind and help release faith with a simple example.

Can you imagine an orange tree having to "believe" to

produce oranges. No, of course not, it knows it's going to produce oranges.

If you asked an orange tree to produce apples, then it would really have to start believing.

An orange tree, by its very nature, must produce oranges. It can't help it.

Before we were Christians, we were barren trees. We could produce no fruit of power. God took hold of us and performed a miracle. He made us born again and changed our very nature. He gave us the gift of the Holy Spirit and the power to produce healing. Now by this very change in our nature, we are a healing tree. By your new nature, you cannot help but produce healings.

Our part is to accept this reality, and renew our minds in this area. Let's stop wasting our faith by asking God for something more.

Simply Branches

We are told in John 15:5: *"I am the vine, you are the branches. He who abides in Me, and I in him, bears much fruit; for without Me you can do nothing."*

Let's get the picture. Jesus the vine inside us, and our arms and hands are the branches. How do a vine and branch work together? All the goodness needed to form the fruit is yielded by the vine. This goodness flows along the branches and fruit is produced.

What is the part played by the branches? They just have to allow the goodness to flow through them.

God uses us as the branches that He flows through to produce fruits of healings at the ends of our hands.

Can you imagine the branch of an orange tree getting

all upset, because it was told it had to produce an orange? Can you see it beginning to panic and have a nervous breakdown as it tries to push and struggle and strain trying to squeeze some fruit out?

We can laugh and say: "What a stupid branch! All it has to do is sit there and the goodness would have flowed through."

Yet today I find many Christians doing the exact same thing. They put their hands on people and push, struggle, grunt and strain trying to "squeeze out" a healing. This is what many call "releasing faith".

Our instruction did not say: "Go and heal them". We were told to go and lay our branches on them. We can be putting our faith in the grunts and groans instead of putting our faith in the vine and His ability to produce the fruit.

God's Little Helpers

We are simply to be the branches and not "God's little helpers" trying to do it in our own strength.

When I was first saved, I was a businessman and I used to have a big silver Mercedes Benz and lived in a penthouse. At that time there were quite a few people trying to get me to go to their particular church. As a young Christian, this was not wise, as I ended up with a false sense of importance. I took pride in the fact that I had so many weekly invitations.

One particular week, a lady invited me to a Pentecostal Church and I went along having no idea what was in store for me. I drove to the church in my Mercedes and walked in in my beautiful three piece suit and lovely shiny shoes, looking immaculate. At that time men's hair spray had just come on to the market and I had heavily sprayed my hair so that it would sit perfectly in place. My hair was so well set, that if you had touched it, you might have broken your fingers. There was I, a proud, well dressed young Christian walking into Church.

At the end of the service, these people began to pray for the sick. I had a slight back pain and moved to the front of the church where some of "God's helpers" were going to get me healed. This particular God's helper, an elderly man, placed his hand right on top of my beautifully set hair style . . . I was not impressed! He began to move his hand back and forth on my head, shaking me and praying. After a rather loud and long prayer lasting a few minutes, he finally finished. I felt like I'd been put through a washing machine. My hair was now standing straight up, pointing in all directions, and I went back to my seat looking like a dazed porcupine.

No, I was not healed. But at least the Lord removed a huge hunk of pride that day.

The man, as good as his heart was, was trying to help God and was trying to get me healed through a method.

The Source

Now where does this idea of shaking come from?

There are times when the power of God can flow through us so strongly that it can shake people. I know, in my early ministry, I had the power of God flow through me so strongly that I could hardly stand up. This manifestation doesn't seem to happen so much today but people still get healed. Perhaps initially God was raising my faith by showing me how divine healing flowed.

There can be times when the power of God can cause you or your hand to shake. However, by observing others doing this and copying it, some Christians have thought that this was the way they should do it. Please don't put your faith in any method. The same kind of problem can arise in another area. Sometimes again, because of the power flowing through, people will fall to the floor. This will not happen to everyone. I have seen some "helping" God by putting their hands on people's foreheads and gently pushing backwards.

There are many places you can lay hands on people. We quite often just hold their hands. If God is leading you to put your hand on their heads, fine, but please don't make a method out of it, and allow God to be God. Remember we are the branches that He is flowing through. If there is a manifestation, then let Him do it. Let's not manufacture it!

Other Person's Faith

Let's now deal with the faith of the person being prayed for. There is a spiritual ingredient that you need to abide by if you are going to receive the healing power:

"Therefore I say to you, whatever things you ask when you pray, BELIEVE THAT YOU RECEIVE them, and you will have them." (Mark 11:24).

So we see faith is needed by the person you are praying for. They need to believe that they receive.

We see this illustrated in Mark 9:23-27 which tells of the story of a man with an epileptic son. The man was desperate when he went to Jesus and said: *"But if you can do anything, have compassion on us and help us."*

Jesus immediately put the ball back in his court and said: *"If you can believe, all things are possible to him who believes."*

The man was obviously shocked by this reply, because now with tears in his eyes, he pleaded: *"Lord, I believe; help my unbelief!"*

What was the man trying to say? It sounds like a complete contradiction. "I believe ... but help my unbelief."

I think he was trying to say: "Lord I am believing with everything I have, but it is not enough. Lord, it takes 100% faith for my boy to be healed, I've got 1% and I know you've got the rest. I believe with my 1%. Help my unbelief with your 99%." That answer bought the needed response from Jesus and the boy was healed.

Why?

Why didn't Jesus simply heal the boy without that conversation? I sense He was trying to find out from the man if he was believing with all he had.

Remember our ingredient is: "Believe that you receive and you shall have." There is an attitude with many people who say: "Oh well, if God wants to heal me, He can." That concept is one of God doing everything, while we lie around and do nothing.

"If He wants to come and heal me, I am available anytime!" It is as silly as saying: "If God wants to save me He can."

Can you imagine trying that attitude out on your local

doctor? As much as his job is to heal you, and he wants to heal you, unless you call him or go to his surgery, you aren't going to get anything.

God expects us to do our part in reaching out to Him for both salvation and healing. Jesus, through His sacrifice, has provided more blessings than found in a doctor's bag. Included in these are eternal life and healing.

He sees mankind is in need and says to them: *"COME TO ME, all you who labour and are heavy laden, and I will give you rest." (Matthew 11:28).*

So what is the basis for healing or any part of the salvation message? People realise they are in need, and then THEY COME to Jesus.

How Much Is Enough?

"How much faith do we have to put forward for healing?" you may be thinking. Answer this question first: "How much faith do you need to be saved and receive eternal life?" Is it 1% or 10%?

It is not possible to put that kind of measurement on faith.

The way that I can best measure it is to call it, "AN OPENESS TO RECEIVE".

Initially your heart would have been hardened towards the things of God. However, you heard the promise of eternal life, opened up your heart and said: "Lord come in." The power of the Holy Spirit flowed in, and a miracle took place. Your heart was changed. You were born again!

How much faith did that take?

With perhaps just a little faith, you opened up your heart.

How does healing work? The same way!

When you hear the message of healing, you merely need to open yourself up. The healing power of the Holy Spirit can flow in, and your body can be healed.

Changing Hard Hearts

Let's try to understand how to get this faith to enter in to the hearts of mankind. If I took a thick piece of timber and tried to put a normal household electric charge through it, I would get a meagre result, because wood is a very poor conductor and has a high resistance to electricity. So it is with men's hearts. They are like wood and hardened towards the things of God. Like the timber, they are resistant to God's power, and so healing and salvation cannot flow in.

Now, if we wanted to see that household power flow through wood, we would have to change the timber into a conducting material like aluminium or brass. This change, however, would require an incredible miracle.

What do we need to do to people whose hearts resist the power of God? We need an incredible miracle to change a resistant heart into one that will allow God's power to flow.

How do we do it?

Remember our previous teaching:

"THE GOSPEL IS THE POWER TO SALVATION".

As we preach it to others, it has the power to change the wooden heart into a conducting heart.

Remember God's word: *"Is alive and full of power - making it active, operative, energizing and effective .."* *(Amp. Hebrews 4:12).*

Once that Gospel power operates on them, they can then turn to the Lord and say: "Lord, I am open to you now. Let your healing power flow in."

Two Faiths Combined

Let us now put together the two faiths.

In the natural, if you had a live electrical wire and connected it to a piece of brass, what must happen? The power would instantly flow through it.

In the spiritual, you simply understand and believe that you are the electric wire carrying God's power, and the believing person is the brass. If you touch them, the power of God must flow through them and then they shall recover.

This is why the Bible is so emphatic. If

1. We preach the Gospel and raise faith;
2. And lay hands upon them;
3. They SHALL recover.

Even Jesus was limited!

Many have a concept that Jesus healed everybody. This is simply not true. He certainly did not heal "all" the ones who had hard hearts.

In His own hometown, Mark 6:5 tells us: *"Now He could do no mighty works there, except that He laid His hands on a FEW sick people and healed them."*

Only a relative few were healed. What happened to all the others? It goes on to tell us in verse 6: *"And He marvelled because of THEIR UNBELIEF."*

To them He was only the carpenter's son, and so they were hard hearted and not open to receive.

In other Scriptures, the Bible says Jesus healed them "ALL". Do we have a contradiction? No, in the records of the other centres, He healed ALL WHO CAME TO HIM. He didn't heal His skeptics, but the ones who came to Him with hearts that said: "Lord we believe you. Heal us."

They ALL received.

The same thing happened to the disciples and was recorded in Hebrews 4:2. Remember we taught earlier: *"For indeed the Gospel was preached to us as well as to them; but the word which they heard did not profit them, not being mixed with faith in those who heard it."*

Teaching - The Answer

God's ingredients certainly do work. The Gospel will raise faith in people. What did Jesus do after the lack of response and unbelief in Nazareth? In Mark 6:6 it says: *"And He marvelled because of their unbelief."* THEN HE WENT ABOUT THE VILLAGES IN A CIRCUIT, TEACHING.

What is the answer to unbelief? Teaching and preaching the Gospel of the Kingdom! With knowledge and understanding of God's word, hardness of heart can be removed. It is no use just saying to both the unsaved or saved: "Just have faith," or "Have more faith." That will not help them. You need to teach and instruct by both Scriptures and experiences of healing that either you or others have had. Faith comes by hearing and hearing and hearing and hearing and hearing the Word of God.

As incredible as it may be, like Jesus, you will from time to time find people who don't want to be prayed for. You see there is that definite qualification for the power of God to flow. The Gospel "*... is the power of God to salvation FOR EVERYONE WHO BELIEVES ...*" Don't be disheartened. Do what Jesus did and help where you can in areas of unbelief, but then go on preaching and teaching to others and see "all" healed in other areas.

Chapter 6

DIFFERENT FAITH LEVELS

We see in Scripture various ways that people received their healing by faith.

Anointing with Oil

In James 5:14 & 15 we are given a specific prayer instruction. As we will see, it confirms the need for faith in both the person praying and the one being prayed for.

"Is anyone among you sick? Let him call for the elders of the Church, and let them pray over him, anointing him with oil in the name of the Lord. And the prayer of faith will save the sick, and the Lord will raise him up."

Again, we are given particular ingredients for this particular healing recipe.

Person's Faith

Notice it does not say for the elders just to go around and pray for anyone who is sick. It says: "Let him (the sick person) call for the elders." What does it tell us about the one in need?

Firstly, we know that they want to be healed and secondly they have determined that if the oil is placed upon them, they are going to be healed. They are acting in faith.

Prayers' Faith

We are then told what is needed to heal: "And the prayer of faith will raise him up."

Faith is also needed by the people praying. Personally, I don't believe you need to be an elder to anoint with oil. In this case elders are used but the focus of the Scripture is on the importance of it being a prayer of faith. If I was very sick, I probably wouldn't want somebody who was saved yesterday praying for me. I would want somebody with deep faith and experience in healing. This is why I believe James instructs us to call for elders. You would expect the elders to be faith people. However, anyone who can pray a prayer of faith can qualify and obviously an elder without faith in this area wouldn't qualify.

Problems can arise when we go in a group to pray for somebody. When they see "Mrs Smith" who is bedridden with cancer, fear can come in and faith can go.

Bob says to himself: "Well, I haven't got any faith but Bill is strong; he'll have the faith!"

Bill says: "Well, I am afraid, but Joan here is a good prayer warrior; she'll have the faith."

Joan thinks: "Well, this is way above my faith level but I am sure these men of God, Bill and Bob, will have what's needed."

Everybody in the group can have faith in somebody else's faith. If you have five people with zero faith, five times zero is zero. There is no safety in numbers. There is only safety in faith. If any one of them had simply relaxed and meditated on Jesus' ability instead of their lack of ability, there would have been faith in the situation.

Cripple Healed

Some people AFTER BEING TAUGHT ON THIS, have great faith for the anointing of oil.

One experience happened in India where a woman, a paraplegic, was seated in the front row of our meeting. I went down to her and noticed she was clutching a small bottle of oil. The Lord told me she was believing for the anointing of oil. I took the bottle from her, put a little on my finger and touched her forehead. I simply said: "Rise, in Jesus' Name."

She instantly rose to her feet, and began to walk. Her face lit up and she threw her hands up in the air and cried out, in her own tongue: "Hallelujah ! Hallelujah!" She then walked back and forth on the platform, with tears streaming down her cheeks, as a witness to all of God's miracle working power.

Fortunately we were able to capture the whole miracle on video and have been able to relive that exciting miracle many times.

Now, if you had been just watching that from a distance, you may have thought: 'Look at that Stuart Gramenz, what a man of power! He raised a cripple!' The truth is, I had little to do with it. The woman had decided in her heart, that if the man puts the oil on me, she would be healed. I was simply a point of contact for her faith to be released.

*This woman was carried into the meeting on a chair —
completely crippled. After anointing of oil she stood and
walked and shed tears of joy.*

How did she get that faith? She obviously had been taught on the anointing with oil.

Faith Levels

We must realise that even after we preach the Gospel, different people will receive different levels of faith. Jesus, realising this, worked to the level of faith that the person actually had. Let's go through some of these varying levels, realising that in each example the faith level to receive gets easier and easier.

1. Hundred Fold Faith

We'll call this hundred fold faith because it is the highest level of faith you can have. Remember when the centurion came to Jesus in Matthew 8 and told Him that his servant was sick. Jesus was willing to go to the household but the man told Him there was no need, and simply said to Jesus: *"But only speak a word, and my servant will be healed."* Jesus marvelled and said: *"Assuredly, I say to you, I have not found such great faith, not even in Israel."*

Only the word was spoken to achieve the healing.

This is exactly what happens when we preach in our crusades.

We preach the Gospel and faith rises in the hearts of the people hearing it. As they sit there listening to the Word they get healed. They didn't need anointing with oil, or laying on of hands. They heard the word only.

As I have been going around and teaching this material the same thing happens. Quite often I get a Word of Knowledge about somebody who has been healed as they listened to the teaching. They have then testified to that fact.

Jesus called it GREAT faith.

However, if I told you all were healed like that it would be totally untrue. Sometimes we get the impression from huge crusades that this is the case. It would be wonderful if it did happen that way, but not everyone in Jesus' day had centurion type faith, and not everyone today has this hundred fold faith.

2. Seventy-Five Fold

Let's go to our next level of faith - seventy five fold. It is demonstrated in Luke 8:43-48, by the woman with the issue of blood. She did not receive by hearing the Word only.

She had obviously heard the good news about Jesus and determined if she could just touch Him, she could be made whole. I call this kind of faith "taking faith". Jesus did not have to lay His hands upon her. She took the power from Jesus, and He felt the power go out from Himself as she touched the hem of His garment.

After we preach the Gospel to large crowds in crusades, there are many who exhibit this "taking", seventy-five fold faith. They press in and just try to touch you. Mothers with little babies will press the babies hand against any part of your body. Again many are healed, but once again all do not have this "taking faith" and all are not healed by this method.

3. Fifty Fold

Something very interesting happened when the woman with the issue of blood reached out and touched Jesus and was healed. Jesus asked a strange question: "Who touched Me?"

It was strange, because at the time, ALL the crowd around Jesus was touching Him. Peter's confused reply was: "Master, the multitudes throng You and press You, and You say 'Who touched Me'?"

Obviously everybody else was pressing in to be healed, but only one touched Him in faith. "Somebody has touched Me, for I perceived power going out of Me," Jesus replied.

Now all the others didn't have "taking faith", but still Jesus healed "ALL" who came to Him. How did He heal the rest?

We now come to our fifty-fold faith level receiving by the laying on of hands. He laid His hands on the rest of the multitude and healed "all" that way.

This is the level where I have found the majority of people are able to release their faith.

We conduct many crusades in third world countries, where we usually take teams of around forty members. This enables us to give personal prayer to every single person.

We may find in crowds of thousands that, say, twenty to thirty are healed by hearing the Word only. But the vast majority then receive their healing by the laying on of hands.

Just think of your own situation. If you were very sick and you wanted somebody to pray for you, you wouldn't just want them to stand ten feet away from you and say: "Be healed!" You would expect them to lay hands on you. Why is this? Because you can release your faith to be healed much more easily by the laying on of hands.

Remember, this is when you are praying for others.

They, like you, in the majority of cases want hands to be laid on them.

I am sure this is why Jesus gave us this specific instruction in our Mark 16 recipe. As much as He realised that many can be healed by other methods, most people relate to being touched and can release their faith that way.

4. Twenty-Five Fold

This principle of being able to receive by touching is further extended in our next level of faith - the anointing with oil.

Through our experience we have noticed that being able to have contact with oil enables the person to receive even more easily than with the other previous forms of prayer.

It is particularly good for very sick people, or those who have little faith.

I believe in James 5 the person who needed to be anointed was a very sick person. It would seem a waste of manpower to send, say, four elders to go to somebody's home. It would make more sense for the person simply to go to them - unless, of course, they are bedridden.

If you are very sick, then your faith level in many cases can drop as well. You need all the help you can get. To have a group of faith-filled people and the anointing with oil can really assist in helping lift your faith once more.

Who is the Healer?

Now, in this teaching we must understand that the OIL CANNOT HEAL.

In 1 Samuel 16:13 we see what actually happened when Samuel anointed David with oil:

"Then Samuel took the horn of oil and anointed him in the midst of his brothers; and the Spirit of the Lord came upon David from that day forward . . .'

The Holy Spirit came upon David.

When we anoint people with oil the Holy Spirit comes upon them and heals them. Obviously the oil doesn't do the healing, but acts as a point of contact to help their faith and receive that power.

Our hands in themselves cannot heal. However, when we lay hands on someone, it is a point of contact to help them believe that they receive.

The hem of a garment or cloths cannot heal. The hem of Jesus' garment was a point of contact. The woman touched it, and believed that she received.

Our words, by themselves, cannot heal.

However, when we preach the Gospel we are not just speaking some words. You are preaching "THE WORD" - God's Words! And as such, they are anointed with power by the Holy Spirit.

What did our teaching in Hebrews 4:12 tell us about the words you are speaking? *"For the Word of God is living and powerful, and sharper than any two-edged sword . . ."*

Remember, our description of the Word in the Amplified Bible. It told us the Gospel you speak is "active, operative, energizing and effective."

The Words of the Gospel are sharper than any sword and go powerfully into men's hearts like an activated lightning bolt.

You may have experienced this energizing, effective

Word hitting you. Perhaps while listening to an anointed teaching, suddenly a particular revelation leapt out at you. You knew the particular Scripture before, but now suddenly it's different. For the first time, you really grasped it deep in your heart. The Word hit you like a bolt and the revelation rose up in your spirit.

After talking to others at the meeting, not everyone shared your enthusiasm. You got something they didn't.

As we preach the Gospel of healing, that lightning of God's Word can touch certain people's hearts. They receive the revelation and are instantly healed.

Don't Be Limited

It is important when preaching to individuals, or to large groups, that you realise there will be different levels of faith in those listening. It will vary from hundred-fold faith to little faith.

Perhaps you are a person with fifty-fold faith. Don't ever limit the listeners to your level of faith. Preach and expect that there will be those who will get the revelation and can be healed from the Word only. Their faith in that particular area will be higher than yours. Also, realise not all are at that level, and then pray and operate at the levels that those of little faith can receive.

Handkerchiefs and Cloths

Let us go on to cover other cases where we can meet the level of faith or situation with effective results.

In some cases the people couldn't come to the meeting, and obviously Paul was unable to get to them. To overcome this difficulty he transferred the healing power through various cloths.

"Now God worked unusual miracles by the hands of Paul, so that even handkerchiefs or aprons were brought from his body to the sick, and the diseases left them and the evil spirits went out of them." (Acts 19:11,12).

Obviously, the handkerchief or apron could not heal, but the anointing power placed there by Paul rested on it until it was received by the person who was sick.

You may have had a build up of static electricity on some of your garments and the power was released onto your hand as you touched it. Similarly the cloths were used as a carrier for the anointing power and then it was released as it was laid upon the person who was to receive.

This is a great way to pray for those who can't attend a meeting, or if it is impossible for you to go personally to them. Simply pray over the handkerchief as you would if the person was there in front of you. That anointing will then rest upon the cloth.

I have also prayed for and anointed other people's hands and had them carry that power to a particular friend or loved one.

In the same way, if you feel the sickness you are praying for is above your faith level, get a man who has the faith, to anoint or empower your hands or the handkerchief, and then go to the person.

Use the Examples

These different faith level prayers have been put in the Bible, not for us to think "My goodness, they prayed in funny ways in those days."

As in Jesus' day, we have people today with varying faith levels.

When you are dealing with individuals, if possible, after preaching the Gospel, teach them the different ways they can receive and let them decide how they wish to be prayed for. If this is not possible, try to work out for yourself what level they are at. Obviously, for most people the easiest levels are with tangible aids such as cloths, oil and hands. They will be the ones used most of the time.

Too often, I have seen situations where a group of Christians in a prayer meeting, home group or church pray for a person who is sick at home. They simply pray: "Lord heal them." In that situation, realise you are trying to operate at hundred-fold centurion level faith. Speak the Word only.

If they are all getting instantly healed, that is excellent; you have a great level of faith. However, I don't believe those kind of results are being achieved by the majority of Christians.

Stop Kneeling For Healing

The principle of asking the Lord to do everything for us while we just go through a certain ritual is not the kind of prayer that heals all.

Perhaps when we heard someone was sick, we just included their name on the end of our prayer list. We clasped our hands together, knelt beside our bed and prayed like the prayer groups: "Lord please heal them."

We are told in Ephesians 6:18 to pray *"with all prayer"*. Another translation says "different kinds of prayer". There are different prayers for different situations. Our example is Jesus. How did He pray for the sick? I can't find one Scripture that tells me He clasped His hands together and knelt beside His bed. I can find many times, where He preached and laid hands on them.

You may feel God has used you in the past to see some healed with prayer, but He wants MORE HEALED, and to do that, we need to make available ALL the methods He used.

Preach the Gospel to those in need, and work to the levels of faith, with the ways we have shown you. I know as you do it that more healings will manifest. Let's stop kneeling for healing and do the works that Jesus did.

Abundant Power

"Now to Him who is able to do exceeding abundantly above all that we ask or think..." (Ephesians 3:20).

Yes, we know God can heal. We know He has all the power, but "somehow" we are not able to get God to release it! That 'somehow' is where you have missed it.

In the Old Covenant, God dwelt in the Holy of Holies in the temple, and people knelt and believed God to move from there. However, we today no longer have to do that. We are under a New Covenant, a better Covenant and God works out of multitudes of New Testament temples.

"Or, do you not know that your body is the temple of the Holy Spirit who is in you..." (1 Corinthians 6:19).

God used to heal from heaven or the temple but now

71

He heals from His new dwelling place - inside you!

Let's go and read the entire Scripture of Ephesians 3:20 that gives us the fulness of what God is trying to tell us.

"Now to Him who is able to do exceeding abundantly above all that we ask or think, ACCORDING TO THE POWER THAT WORKS IN US."

God can do above anything we ask or think - exceeding abundantly, if we release the power that is within us.

In New Zealand a woman came forward for prayer. She wished to give birth to more children. Because of infection, one of her fallopian tubes had been removed surgically. The other had since become affected in the same way.

We laid hands on her, believing that the infection would clear up in the one remaining tube.

The woman, unsure of her healing, went ahead with her surgery appointment. During the operation the doctors were amazed to find that not only had the infected tube cleared up, but the one that had been previously removed by them had grown back! She experienced a complete restoration miracle - much more than we had asked for!

Practitioners have told me since that it was a medical impossibility for this tube to grow again.

We serve a God who is able to do much more than we dare to think or ask, through the power that He has placed IN US.

Chapter 7

THEY SHALL RECOVER

We now come to the third ingredient of our recipe in Mark 16.

Remember our first two ingredients:

1. Preach the Gospel; 2. Lay hands on the sick; and if we do these things according to our instruction, the third part of our recipe will occur: "They shall recover."

Note, the Bible does not say if you lay hands on the sick they will be instantly healed.

If you went to the doctor and he said, "take these pills and you shall recover," you are not expecting to be healed immediately after you swallow the first one. Recovery implies a time period. The N.I.V. translates it: "They will get well."

Although in most cases recorded, the people recovered within a few seconds, there are some cases when the recovery time has taken longer.

Luke 17:12-14 is the story of ten lepers. Jesus told them to go and show themselves to the priests.

"And IT CAME TO PASS AS THEY WENT, they were cleansed."

They were healed "as they went!" In other words, a period of time elapsed.

In the story of the nobleman's son in John 4:49-53, Jesus told the man that his son would live. Returning home, the man talked to his servants. The King James version says: *"Then inquired he of them THE HOUR*

WHEN HE BEGAN TO AMEND." J.B. Phillips translates it: "He asked them at what time he had begun to recover." The boy did not just jump out of his bed and begin playing football. He BEGAN TO GET BETTER from the hour that Jesus declared him well.

We have found God healing different people in different ways. For instance, we prayed for ten deaf and dumb children. Nine were healed instantly; the other one recovered the next day.

Why does God do it this way?

Well, we don't know all the answers, but the important thing is to realise that "THEY SHALL RECOVER".

Nothing Happened!

A problem can arise for us if we are not aware of the recovery ingredient. Imagine if you preached the Gospel to someone, laid hands on them and then asked them in faith: "How are you now?"

The person replies: "The pain is still there - NOTHING HAPPENED!"

Your faith can sink along with theirs, unless you understand the ingredient of recovery.

"Nothing happened!" has killed the faith of a lot of people who should have recovered. No wonder the Lord said *"My people are destroyed through lack of knowledge."*

What To Do

Immediately when somebody says to me, "Nothing happened!" a little alarm goes off in my spirit. I won't and can't receive that nothing has happened.

Now I agree that the pain is still there. This is not a mind over matter situation, where we are trying to heal the person by saying:

"The pain is not there!

The pain is not there!"

The pain is there. But to say "nothing happened" would be equally untrue.

If you have preached to them and they are open to receive, like the example of the electricity and brass, they will conduct that healing power.

When you lay hands on a person who is open to receive, something happens ...

THE "ELECTRICAL" POWER OF THE HOLY SPIRIT FLOWS IN!

Now, because they have a lack of understanding in spiritual matters, they may not be aware that power has flowed in. In their ignorance all they can say is: "Nothing happened!"

Parable of the Doctor

Now we have two truths here:

1. The healing power has gone in;
2. The pain is still there.

To help them to understand this spiritual truth, I tell people of the parable of the doctor.

You know the doctor has knowledge of your body and has an ability to administer healing. Because of this, you can trust him and are willing to follow his directions.

God knows more about your body than any doctor. Why? He designed you and knows exactly what is needed to make you well.

75

After diagnosing the problem, a doctor may give you a prescription. He tells you: "Take 3 pills a day for the next 4 days and you shall recover."

God has a prescription also. He tells us: "Lay hands on the sick and they shall recover."

When you take the first pill from the doctor, do you expect to be healed instantly? No! You don't race back down to his surgery and say: "Nothing happened, I want my money back!"

You understand that once that pill goes into your body, its power begins to operate. If you allow the pill to do its work, you shall recover, just as the doctor promised.

When we pray for people, a "pill" of God's power goes into their body. A "Gos-pill". It begins a work and will continue to do so. You don't need to be prayed for 3 times a day for the next 5 days. You receive the entire course in one powerful dosage.

You simply now have to relax and allow the power of God to do its work, and you shall recover.

Believe You Receive

We must ensure the person being prayed for understands this principle. The Bible says: *"When you pray (for things) believe that you receive them, and you will have them." (Mark 11:24).*

If we looked at this Scripture conversely, it means if the person does not believe they have received that healing power pill, then they shall not receive that healing.

Confess with Your Mouth

We are told one of the principles to receive eternal life

is to *"confess with your mouth ... and believe with your heart"* (Romans 10:9).

Similarly, the same principle applies to this healing portion of your salvation.

"...And with the mouth confession is made to salvation" (verse 10).

Not realising this spiritual truth of recovery can have you believing in your heart, "nothing happened". This can lead to automatically confessing with your mouth nothing happened. Your negative faith and negative confession can lead to the neutralizing of God's healing power.

This is one reason why I believe so many Christians and non Christians alike have "lost" potential healings.

Give It Time

We live in a time of fast food, instant coffee and, of course, there is a desire to get an instant miracle. If the doctor tells you that you would be well in five days, can you imagine yourself stamping your feet getting upset and saying "but I want it now?"

With Jesus' power, you can be healed much faster than by medical help, but can we give Doctor Jesus at least as much time as we do our normal doctor. If you just relax and allow the healing power to work, you may be surprised at how quickly you are healed.

I'm obviously not saying that every person is going to be a recovery case. We have discovered the great majority of people are healed within a minute. Even within that minute people with exactly the same complaints recover at different rates. Some are healed in ten seconds, others thirty seconds and so on.

Again we may ask: "Why is it so?" Again we haven't all the answers, but we do know God's promise: "They shall recover!"

Extra Hindrances

In terminal cases such as cancers and tumours, we have had situations where people instantly felt some change. However, we have found the majority of these to be recovery cases.

Apart from the normal "recovery" faith which is needed by these people, we find ourselves quite often dealing with an extra obstacle. After a visit to the doctor, a person may be told, for example, that they have 6 months to live. What happens to most people in this position?

FEAR FLOODS IN!

Now, this fear can be quite obvious sometimes while others manage to hide it. Naturally, most people fear death.

"Christians would not be afraid to die," you may be thinking.

You may be surprised about that!

If a person is not fearing for themselves, they may be fearing for the welfare of their family. Who is going to look after the husband or the wife and who will raise the children?

Fear and Faith Are Opposites!

If faith aids healing, what does fear do? It assists the disease to kill and destroy.

I know the reality of this situation, as both my father

and uncle died of cancer. They were going through a very slow deterioration in their bodies and visited the doctor. When he told them they had cancer, then suddenly their condition, worsened dramatically.

My father in particular died even in a much shorter period of time than the doctor had given him. I know many other cases where a similar thing has occurred - gradual decline in the person, and then sudden worsening. The reason for this in many cases is fear.

Unfortunately, as a very young Christian, without the knowledge or faith I have today, I had to stand by, helplessly, and do nothing.

I am sure there are some reading this now, who are trying to work out why certain loved ones died. The purpose of the book is not to dig into the past, but to give you knowledge and faith to stop cancer and other diseases stealing the lives of others in the future.

Put Them In The Picture

We have found, as with the parable of the doctor, giving the sick insight into what is actually happening in the spirit realm, gives them a stronger faith. With cancer victims, I tell the story found in Mark 11:12-24. In this Scripture Jesus curses a fig tree. We know whenever Jesus spoke, something dramatic happened. Lepers were cleansed. The blind saw. The cripples walked.

But to the dismay of His disciples, nothing apparently happened to the tree. It looked just the same. When they passed by the tree again next morning, Peter was amazed to find that the tree was withering away.

Most importantly, they noticed that IT HAD

SHRIVELLED FROM THE ROOTS UP.

When Jesus cursed it, He did not speak to the branches. He talked to the source - the roots!

When did the tree actually die? When Jesus spoke to it. It wasn't obvious at that point because the disciples couldn't see the root. They could only believe something had happened when the branches began to wither.

We could think perhaps they lacked faith and should have been able to believe what Jesus had said. However, today's disciples suffer a similar problem. We seem to believe only what we actually see.

Cancer starts as a root somewhere, and then branches through the body. We don't see the cancer. We see the branches - the sickly and weak appearance of the person.

Many of us, when praying for sufferers, can make the mistake of only trying to kill the branches. We can only believe the cancer root is dead when we see the branches are dead.

At the end of a prayer session, if the person doesn't look or feel any better, we feel we have failed. Your negative faith and attitude can be picked up by the person you are praying for.

When we are dealing with cancer, we are not interested in the branches only, but the root. We can curse the root. We pray like this: "Cancer, I command you to die. Go out now, in the name of Jesus Christ!"

The power of God can then go in and kill the root of the cancer.

Once the root is dead, what must eventually happen to the branches? They must die as well.

Explaining this process to the person, will give them faith and fear can be automatically removed.

Two Case Histories

1. Here is part of a testimony of a young woman we prayed for:

"After a doctor's examination, I was astonished to be told I had an ovarian cyst the size of a golf ball. It had surrounded my whole ovary, cutting off the blood supply and turning it poisonous. I went to a radiologist for an ultra sound X-Ray and she could see immediately through the machine that there was one on the left and one on the right, both the size of golf balls. My heart sank a little at the possibility of losing both ovaries and any future family.

"After leaving the doctor's surgery, I began to confess the Word of God. Jesus told us that all we have to do is believe. I was trusting in Jesus, so I kept confessing and believing it.

"Stuart and Mary Gramenz had agreed to pray for me on the Thursday night and I was to see the doctor on the Friday morning.

"Stuart talked to me about the unfruitful fig tree, and how Jesus cursed it, and how it died from the roots up. He said that was what the cysts were going to do; they were going to dry up from the very root. He and Mary then laid hands on me and prayed.

"Next day I arrived at the doctor's surgery very happy and very peaceful. We looked at the X-Ray, now back from the radiologist, and in the natural, the situation had grown worse. It showed that on my right ovary there were actually two cysts, the size of golf balls, a total of three large cysts!

"Despite the X-Ray, I knew that once the doctor examined me he would find no cysts, and that, praise God, is exactly what happened.

"The doctor, who was not a Christian, stood shaking his head. He just couldn't explain it! Some three-quarters of an hour later, the doctor was convinced that there was probably a God, and he admitted that there was no medical explanation. He also said that he couldn't argue that there had been a 'supernatural intervention'!"

2. A pastor's wife came to us with a lump in her womb the size of a 3-month-old foetus. Her doctor wanted her to undergo emergency surgery within a few days. We, along with others, prayed and cursed that lump.

Being unsure of the result, she underwent the surgery and the doctor couldn't find a trace of it!

We have seen all kinds of lumps, tumours and other afflictions healed by this method. We have a God who keeps His Word:

"THEY SHALL RECOVER..."

If we can only believe it

Chapter 8

PRAYING MORE THAN ONCE

"Can we pray for people more than once?" is a question asked by many.

Let's once again look at Mark 11:24

"Therefore I say to you, whatever things you ask when you pray, believe that you receive them, and you will have them."

"If we pray and believe we receive them, we shouldn't have to pray again," many might argue.

Our example in all things is Jesus. Was there any time that Jesus prayed more than once? He did in a story found in Mark 8:22-25 when He prayed for a blind man. Jesus *"put His hands on him"*. The man said: *"I see men like trees, walking."* In other words, he was beginning to see - he was recovering.

It goes on to say: *"Then He put His hands on his eyes again and made him look up."*

What happened as a result of this second prayer? *"And he was restored and saw everyone clearly."*

There is a great difference here, between the concept that many Christians have of praying more than once, and the repeated prayer of Jesus.

Try, Try Again!

In many cases Christians have prayed once, assumed nothing had happened, and then felt they must try, try,

try, again.

Jesus did not pray the second time because nothing happened with His first prayer. The power of God did flow in and he was recovering, he was beginning to see.

Jesus prayed the second prayer not because He thought: "I've missed the first time, I'd better have another go."

His second prayer brought the recovery to its completion.

Divine healing is not like buying some ticket in a lottery, with the thought that if you buy a ticket week after week, your number will eventually come up. There have been many people who have gone from meeting to meeting, person to person, waiting for their instant prize.

If you are a person who is going to be healed by recovery and yet each time you are prayed for never "believe and receive", you won't be healed. You will simply be nullifying any power that goes into you each time with your doubt that says:

"Nothing happened...again."

People who do not understand the principle can give up, and assume that God does not want to heal them.

It is also important to know that just because you received an "instant" healing last time, it doesn't mean you are going to have the same now. You can be healed over seconds, minutes, hours or days.

Physical Evidence

In this case because the man was blind, we had

physical evidence that recovery was taking place. What if he had a tumour and you couldn't see that he was being healed? Would it mean that God's power wasn't flowing in? Of course not.

This is a great example to show us the principle of recovery and we must have the same faith whether we can see the recovery or not.

Spirit Led

Jesus was always led by the Father, and there may be times when you are led like Him to bring the healing through to completion.

Why did Jesus pray twice in this situation? I can't say for sure. Perhaps in this case, the man may not have had high faith. If left with only partial sight, he may not have been able to believe for total recovery, or perhaps he may have even lost what he had.

Maybe Jesus sensed this and brought the healing through to its fulness to avoid that problem. I know in our own ministry we have had times when we were led to bring the healing through.

We were street preaching in Auckland and made an appeal for the sick to come forward. A woman who was completely blind in one eye, stepped up and I began to pray for her. She then covered her good eye and realised that she could see the outlines of people. I prayed again and this time she could make out the men from the women. The third prayer resulted in exact detailing of articles of clothing, colours of ties and so on. She became excited and wept for joy.

I was led by the Spirit to pray more than once. Perhaps,

if I had only prayed the once, over the next few days she may have recovered. I believe the reason for the three healing prayers that night, was because of the unbelievers present. Most of them would have been skeptical anyway. Their thinking may have been "half a miracle is no miracle." Seeing the reality of her gradually being healed and the joy at the end of it, certainly had an impact on them, and they came forward for further counselling.

A Practical Second Prayer

What do we do with people who we prayed for last week, and are still sick this week?

For instance, Bill came to our meeting with malignant cancer, we gave him the Gospel, told him how to receive. We are believing for his recovery but his healing has still not manifested.

Bill has contacted us, his faith is wavering and he wants us to pray again. Do we pray a second time? and if so how do we pray?

Many people we have prayed for at meetings can go back into negative home environments. For example, Bill goes home all excited that the root of cancer has been cursed. His faith is very high. His well meaning, but untaught wife, has one look at him and says: "Bill you look terrible, let me help you into bed." His well wishing friends visit him the next day, trying to "help" him in every way they can. "Hi, Bill, is there anything we can do for you before...um...you know...er...you leave us."

The doctor, friends and relatives are constant reminders of the "fact" you are going to die.

Remember FEAR and FAITH are opposing forces - they are enemies.

FAITH comes by hearing and hearing by the Word of God.

FEAR comes by hearing and hearing the word of man.

If they are in a negative environment, surrounded by doctors, friends and relatives, they will be constantly reminded of the "facts" - "you are going to die!"

You must create a positive environment and surround them with the word of God and constant reminders of His promise: "You shall recover."

Whatever they hear, hear, and hear they are going to have faith for.

Praising Faith

We can learn of how to wait for the results of God's promise by looking at Abraham. He was promised a son, but that boy wasn't born immediately. However because God had promised him, Abraham had faith in God's word. The Amplified Bible says in Romans 4:20 *"No unbelief or distrust made him waver or doubtingly question concerning the promise of God..."*

We today have a promise equal to that son, a promise that we will give birth to a healing and we "shall recover". No unbelief or distrust should make us doubt His word.

How did Abraham maintain this strong faith through the long waiting period?

Romans 4:20 goes on to tell us: *"... But he grew strong and was empowered by faith and he gave praise and glory to God."*

What was the reason he had strong empowered faith?

He gave praise and glory to God!

I have noticed among some Christians, a lack of understanding of how to praise God in a difficult situation. It does not mean you run around in circles at a prayer meeting or in your house, yelling out: "Praise God! Praise God! Praise God! Hallelujah! Hallelujah! Hallelujah!"

It means 1. Reading God's promise;
2. Seeing yourself receive that promise;
3. Thanking Him for that result

If Abraham lived today, I think I know what he would do if he was promised a son. He would go down to the shops and immediately buy a cot, children's clothes, paint the nursery blue and set up all the new toys around the room.

He would then start thinking of all the things he was going to do with his son, and begin to thank God: "Oh Lord, I thank You for my boy, it's going to be really great, playing football with him and taking him out fishing with me. I praise You, Lord. You've answered the prayer of my heart. Thank You Lord, I give You all the praise and glory."

What do you think happens as he pictures the promises that God was going to give him. His faith increases even more; "Abraham grew strong and was empowered by faith as he gave praise and glory to God."

Our Faith

Do we want our faith to be strong and empowered so

that we can give birth to healings? We must learn and use the principles of Abraham.

We have a promise today. The same God that said to Abraham: "You shall have a son," is the same God that says to us who believe: "You shall lay hands on the sick and they shall recover."

No unbelief or distrust should make us waver or doubtingly question concerning that promise.

So how do we pray for Bill, the second time? We lay our hands on him and say: "Father God, we thank You that Your healing power entered Bill's body last week and has destroyed the root of that cancer. We praise You that moment by moment, day by day, the branches of that cancer are withering and that every affected cell is being healed. We thank You that once again Bill is going to come to church again. We can see him going out with his wife, playing with the children and recommencing his work.

"We thank You Lord for Your promise to him and thank You for his healing."

We are not nullifying last week's faith prayer but thanking God for His continuing work and also at the same time building faith in Bill and crushing fear and doubt.

If Bill is continually having a faith battle, I would pray for him as many times as possible. If you can't get to him, ring him up, and have him put his hands on the worst area and pray the same prayer.

Bill's Faith in Action

After a few days, Bill will catch onto the heart of the prayer. You can say to him "Bill would you like to grow strong and have your faith more empowered?"

"How do I do that?" he may ask.

"Simply lay your hands on yourself and pray the same prayer that I've been praying:

"Thank You Lord, Your healing power is in me. Moment by moment You are healing every part of my body. I thank You I am going to be able to do all the things I did before. I can see myself giving my testimony to others of the wonderful work You have done in me, and Jesus, I praise You for it."

If Bill is at home, he will have little else to do anyway. He can spend most of the day praising and glorifying God. His faith will become empowered. As he is hearing now more and more of God's Word instead of man's, fear of death will be forced out of his heart.

Mind Over Matter?

Some have thought that this kind of confession borders on positive thinking or mind over matter.

Others wanting to speak only the truth, have felt they may be saying something they feel is not real.

This is not mind over matter or speaking untruth.

Let's imagine a Christian woman who has been pregnant for three months. No one can really tell yet. She looks just the same. If at that time she went around declaring: "I'm going to have a baby, would you call that mind over matter? Would you say, she is speaking an untruth. The woman knows it to be a fact.

Just because we can't see the baby doesn't mean it is not on the way.

When you come in contact with Jesus, a seed of His

power begins a work in your body. You can, without any problem, like the pregnant woman, say "I'm going to have a healing."

It is not an untruth. In fact, just the opposite - it is working and confessing in line with the truth that God's power is birthing in your body.

Know the Difference

There is a gulf of difference between the devil's counterfeit of healing through mind dynamics, and God's power through His Son. The devil will always try to give glory to man, puffing him up and making him think he is the centre of all things.

With divine healing, the power is not in a mind, it is in a Person. Divine healing will always glorify the Son, Jesus Christ.

If healing is not giving glory to Him, be wary of it.

Parable Of the Band-aid

Our final parable in this chapter will help us remember the importance of praise.

Imagine if you cut your hand and didn't attend to it. After a while it could become totally infected.

How would you treat it?

First, of all you would clean the wound and put antiseptic on it. The antiseptic kills the bacteria, the root of the problem, and then the wound can heal.

When we pray, the power of God works like the antiseptic. It goes in and kills the root of the problem. The affliction then has the potential to recover. After you have put the antiseptic on your wound, you don't leave the wound open and go and work in the garden or fix the car. With no protection, it will become re-infected. You need to put a covering on it. A band-aid placed over the wound will stop the dirt and bacteria from entering in.

What is the spiritual equivalent of dirt and bacteria? FEAR AND DOUBT!

If the enemy can get enough fear and doubt into you, your healing faith can be nullified, and the healing "re-infected."

How do these thoughts and words of fear and doubt come in? Through your mind.

You have to place a spiritual band-aid over your ears to keep the bacteria of fear and doubt out.

What is our spiritual band-aid? PRAISE !

As we praise God, it acts as a spiritual force to ward off fear and doubt.

Here is an example of how it may work.

Bacteria: Nothing happened - you still look the same.

You: Thank You Jesus, Your healing power is in me.

Bacteria: Give up, the pain is still there.

You: Thank You Lord, moment by moment I am recovering.

Bacteria: You've been prayed for before, nothing happened then, nothing will happen now.

You: I've received the healing power of God, I'm pregnant with it. Thank You Jesus.

Bacteria: You are not a good person; you don't deserve it.

You: On the cross He died for my sins and by His stripes I am healed. Oh, I praise You God.

Bacteria: Forget this person, they're too tough; we can't get through.

As we continue to keep our spiritual band-aid of resistance, the devil with all his doubts and fears will leave us.

"RESIST THE DEVIL AND HE WILL FLEE FROM YOU." (James 4:7).

If you keep your band-aid over your cut long enough, one day you will look under it and be able to declare: "It is all better."

If we keep our band-aid of praise on long enough, you'll finally be able to declare: "I'm totally healed."

Faith In Your Praise

It is so important for us to understand the reason we praise God, and the power generated through it.

I've prayed for hundreds of people at our meetings, knowing that the power of healing went into them. A few moments later, they have come to me very concerned, with those now familiar words: "Nothing happened!"

In these situations it is impossible to give hours of teaching every night on receiving and recovery. I and other evangelists are forced into giving a very hurried instruction such as, "just keep thanking the Lord", or "keep saying, by His stripes I am healed."

There is obviously truth in this. They must, however, understand the principle of the faith behind the praise.

They could be thinking: "If I just say this hundreds of times this week, I'll get my healing."

They are putting their faith in repeating the words instead of faith in the Healer.

"But when you pray, do not use vain repetitions as the heathen do. For they think that they will be heard for their

many words." (Matthew 6:7).

Ever present is the concept: "Well nothing happened when he prayed for me today, but if I just keep saying the words some day in the future, God may touch me."

They still haven't grasped the truth that God's healing power flowed into them today. They still have to grasp the truth of "believe you receive and you shall have", and realise they were pregnant with the healing the moment they were touched.

That is why I now spend more time on teaching these principles, so that more people are not destroyed through lack of knowledge.

Learn these keys and teach them to others.

Chapter 9

IT'S WHAT'S DOWN UNDER THAT COUNTS

We now look at our second "recipe" for healing and more spiritual ingredients that will help us.

Acts 3:6-8 tells the story of a cripple who was raised through the apostle Peter: *"Then Peter said: 'Silver and gold I do not have, but what I do have I give you; In the name of Jesus Christ of Nazareth, rise up and walk.' And he took him by the right hand and lifted him up, and immediately his feet and ankle bones received strength. So he, leaping up, stood and walked and entered the temple with them - walking, leaping and praising God."*

In this passage we have four more ingredients that will help us release the power of God.

The first ingredient is the realisation of the power that is within us: "Silver and gold I do not have, BUT WHAT I DO HAVE I give to you."

Money wasn't going to help him to be healed, but he had something else. He had the power of the Holy Spirit which filled him on the day of Pentecost.

Jesus Power

I have found that one of the greatest deterrents to people releasing faith is their lack of understanding of the power they have. That is why, although we have covered some teaching in this area in earlier chapters, we need to build more faith by hearing and hearing more of it.

I know when I first read John 14:12 telling me I could do the works that Jesus did, I felt inhibited.

"Me do what Jesus did? Oh No!" I thought. After all He was the Son of God, and you expect the Son of God to do great things.

Surely no one could do what Jesus did?

I soon realised that I was not the one who said I could do His works. Jesus said it!

Either He is playing a joke with the Church or He meant what He said. I know Jesus doesn't play games with us. He meant every word. If He said we could do His works, then He must have made a way possible for us to do them.

Many of us make wrong assumptions. We assume that Jesus did all His miracle healings because He was the Son of God.

Let's make one thing very clear, Jesus was unable to move in signs and wonders precisely BECAUSE He was the Son of God!

The Amplified Bible tells us about Jesus, who: *"Stripped Himself (of all privileges and rightful dignity) so as to assume the guise of a servant (slave), in that, He became like men and was born a human being." (Philippians 2:7)*

Jesus came to earth as the Son of God, BUT without any of His miracle working powers.

I'm sure you already realise that anyway.

At the age of 10, was He the Son of God? Yes!

Was He Healing the sick? No!

At the age of 16, was He the Son of God? Certainly!

Was He walking on water? No!

At the age of 21, was He the Son of God? Definitely!

Was He forgiving sin? No!
At the age of 29, was He the Son of God? Naturally!
Was He casting out demons? No!
All this time He was the sinless Son of God, but had
stripped Himself of all power.

How Did He Heal?

Something happened to change His life dramatically.
When He was "about thirty years of age", the Bible
tells us in Luke 3:21-22, He was baptized in water
and was filled with the Holy Spirit.

As a result of this event, His ministry of healing
began and He became a talking point in the
area.

*"Then Jesus returned in the power of the Spirit to Galilee,
and news of Him went out through all the surrounding
region". (Luke 4:14).*

Why wasn't there news of Jesus before this? Because
He was unable to minister or heal without the "power
of the Spirit". He even confirmed this immediately
in Luke 4:18: *"The Spirit of the Lord is upon Me,"*
He declared.

Which Spirit? The Holy Spirit, of course!

Now why had the Holy Spirit come upon Him?
"Because He (the Holy Spirit) *has anointed Me to preach
the Gospel to the poor. He has sent Me to heal the broken
hearted, to preach to the captives, and recovery of sight to
the blind."*

The word "anointed" means "empowered". Jesus was
empowered by the Holy Spirit to do every aspect of His
ministry.

97

Powerful Preaching

I always thought that Jesus was a great preacher because He was the Son of God.

NO! HE WAS A GREAT PREACHER BECAUSE HE WAS THE SON OF GOD, EMPOWERED BY THE HOLY SPIRIT.

Even in His preaching of the Gospel, it was the power of the Spirit operating. I'm sure most of us are already aware that it is the Holy Spirit who convicts the unsaved.

Casting Out Demons

Some of us have been under a misapprehension about casting out demons. You may have thought that only Jesus could handle the real tough ones. No! If that was the case, John 14:12 where says we can do His works would be wrong. How did Jesus cast out demons? Was it solely based on His authority as the Son of God? He tells us Himself:

"If I cast out demons BY THE SPIRIT OF GOD surely the Kingdom of God has come upon you." (Matthew 12:28).

He again used the power of the Holy Spirit. We can see that Jesus' ministry of preaching, healing, and casting out demons was performed through the releasing of the power given to Him in the river Jordan, when the Holy Spirit descended upon Him.

Same Power for Us

This same power was available to Peter and every believer. Jesus promised them: *But you shall receive power when the Holy Spirit has come upon you." (Acts 1:8).*

Many had thought previously that this power was only for those few disciples, but Peter tells us clearly: "You shall receive the gift of the Holy Spirit. For the promise is to you and to your children, and to all who are afar off, AS MANY AS THE LORD OUR GOD WILL CALL." (Acts 2:38, 39).

Has He called you? Then you are included in this promise to receive the gift of the Holy Spirit. If you are filled with the Holy Spirit, you have a gigantic, dynamic power, waiting to be used.

Be Filled Now

If you are not filled, or sense the lack of power in your life, you can pray this prayer right now and loud:
"Dear Lord, I want to fulfil
my role of praying for the sick, and I
realise my lack of ability.
You promised that each disciple - including me,
could receive that empowerment from on high.
Fill me, Holy Spirit. Thank you Lord,
I receive that empowerment to set others free
right now, and I praise you for it."
With that simple prayer, the Holy Spirit has empowered you for miracle working service.

Let's Imitate Elisha

Let's look at an Old Testament example of how God expects us to act after receiving the anointing.

2 Kings 2:8-14 tells of Elijah and his servant Elisha. Elijah was a great prophet who performed many miracles, including raising the dead and calling fire down from heaven.

Here he is about to be taken to heaven.

Jesus, our Master, was also taken up into heaven.

Elijah told his disciple, Elisha, that if he saw him taken up, a double portion of his spirit would rest upon Elisha. (Verse 9-10).

The story is very similar to Jesus, who promised His disciples: *"...The works that I do he will do also; and greater works than these ye will do, because I go to my Father." (John 14:12).*

The "greater works" portion has been promised to Jesus' disciples. Earlier in 2 Kings 2:8, it tells how Elijah had used his mantle to separate the waters of the river Jordan:

"Now Elijah took his mantle, rolled it up, and struck the water; and it was divided this way and that, so that the two of them crossed over on dry ground."

The mantle of Elijah was a type of the anointing of the Holy Spirit. Elijah did his part in the miracle, and the Holy Spirit did the rest. We saw how Jesus used "His mantle" His anointing of the Holy Spirit, to perform the miracles.

"How God anointed Jesus of Nazareth with the Holy Spirit and with power, who went about doing good and healing all who were oppressed by the devil, for God was with Him." (Acts 10:38).

He could "do nothing of Himself." He said quite often that He relied on the Father for direction, and that the power to perform the miracles came from the Holy Spirit.

If this is the way Jesus performed His "works", then surely we should be doing ours the same way. Elisha knew he could do nothing of himself. When Elijah's mantle fell as he ascended, Elisha immediately tore up his own clothes. He had known Elijah's ability to move in the supernatural and would have to rely on what his master had left him. He discarded his own things, and took up the old mantle of Elijah.

As disciples today, we have the "mantle" of God's anointing. How did Elisha use his mantle to operate the supernatural? He went straight back to the river Jordan to follow the example given by his master Elijah.

"Then he took the mantle of Elijah that had fallen from him, and struck the water, and said: *"Where is the Lord God of Elijah?" And when he also had struck the water, it was divided this way and that; and Elisha crossed over." (2 Kings 2:14).*

The mantle wasn't some new mantle, or one with lesser power. It was exactly the same mantle that Elijah had used. Elisha knew what he had - he knew the power of that mantle, and he went out and used it.

The mantle that Peter received was not some new mantle or part of a mantle. He knew what he had. He went out and used it:

"Silver and gold I do not have, but what I do have I give you: In the name of Jesus Christ of Nazareth, rise up and walk."

What was he doing? Following the example of his Master, Jesus! Elisha called on the God of Elijah. Peter called on the name of Jesus Christ.

TODAY WE NEED TO REALISE THAT JESUS CHRIST HAS HANDED HIS MANTLE TO US. IT IS NOT SOME NEW MANTLE, BUT THE SAME "OLD"

MANTLE THAT ENABLED JESUS CHRIST TO DO HIS WORKS.

God is now looking for the Church to catch the same spirit of Elisha, and rise up to strike the devil, using the mantle entrusted to it.

Wrong Pictures

I know that as a small child attending Sunday School, I picked up many wrong concepts which later affected my ability to believe that I had a great power within me.

I remember one day my Sunday School teacher telling me that Jesus dwelt in my heart. My immediate picture was Jesus, the size of a mouse, living inside me. I was also told that He could help me when I had any problems. I used to get into a lot of trouble, but I had difficulty believing a midget-sized Jesus could help me. Many of us have a similar, wrong concept. We know Jesus in heaven is powerful and strong, but we lack the same belief for the Jesus now dwelling in us.

Naturally, when we receive the power of the Holy Spirit, the same problem can arise. Our mind pictures a huge powerful Holy Spirit in the heavenlies, but just a little power actually in us.

Once He comes upon you, His power enables you to perform two levels of power ministry.

First of all, it enables you to duplicate the ministry of Jesus preaching, laying hands on the sick and casting out demons, as told to us in Mark 16.

Secondly, "as He wills" you will be able to move in certain Gifts of the Spirit listed in 1 Corinthians 12:8-11.

Treasure Within

We must grasp the truth of what God has placed within us. Paul said that we have this *"treasure in earthen vessels"*. *(2 Corinthians 4:7).*

When I think of treasure, I imagine gold, silver, precious jewels. God has placed a spiritual treasure within you.

In Paul's day, there were all kinds of vessels, made of different materials. The least expensive of these would have been the earthen one. A modern day translation would be "a treasure in a paper cup."

J.B. Phillips translates the full scripture:

"The priceless treasure we hold, so to speak, in common earthenware - to show the splendid power of it belongs to God and not of us."

In comparison to the priceless treasure that is in you, your body is like a paper cup. Remember this comparison when you are praying, so that you are relying on the contents and not the container.

Priceless Treasure

Why is this treasure priceless?

If you lay your hands on a cripple, and that treasure flows into his body, and heals him? What price can you put on those healthy legs ?

If you lay hands on a blind person, and the treasure flows into his eyes and he is healed? What price can you put on restored sight ?

If a barren woman after ten years of marriage, receives that treasure, and gives birth within a year. Parents, what price can you put on your children?

The treasure that God has placed within you, cannot have an earthly value placed on it.

Buried Treasure

If God gave you a million dollars to help the hurting people in the world, would you bury it?

He has placed within you the priceless treasure of the Holy Spirit's power to help others in this world. Yet unwittingly, many have left this power buried inside them.

Jesus gave a command to His disciples which still applies for us today: *"And as you go, preach, saying: 'The kingdom of heaven is at hand'. Heal the sick, cleanse the lepers, raise the dead, cast out demons. Freely you have received, freely give." (Matthew 10:7,8).*

What did He freely give to them?

The treasure of the Holy Spirit.

What were they to do with it?

Give to those who were needy.

That is what Peter did to the cripple. *"Silver and gold I do not have, but SUCH AS I HAVE I GIVE TO YOU."*

He gave that man the priceless treasure of the Holy Spirit, and saw him healed.

That Holy Spirit power is lying dormant in you right now. Make a commitment to God that you are going to dig it up and begin to distribute it to those who are in need!

God's Banking System

In the early days of our present large cities, there would

have initially been one bank. That bank kept all the money in its treasury and distributed it to those who needed to draw on it.

When Jesus came to earth, initially all the heavenly treasure was kept with Him and He would distribute it as it was needed.

As a town grows, it is impossible for all the people to go to the central bank. Firstly, there are too many people for the one bank to service. Secondly, it may be impossible or inconvenient to come a long distance. To solve this problem, the head office opens a network of branch offices connected to it, and gives them authority to meet people's needs and give out money, exactly the same way head office does.

Jesus came to meet the needs of an entire world. Obviously, one man could not pray for everyone, and ALL the people in the world certainly could not get to Him.

To solve the problem, Jesus set up a plan to have "branches" in every suburb in every town in the world. The Holy Spirit gives each branch a deposit of treasure for them to distribute.

You are God's "branch" in the area where you live, and you have been commissioned to distribute to those in need. You are a chosen generation, a special people chosen to do this task.

Running out of Power

If a bank branch office runs out of money, it simply contacts head office, and the supply is replenished.

As we distribute the Holy Spirit treasure of power, we

need to be always in contact with our Head Office to ensure we always have ample in our vaults.

This is what happened to Peter. In Acts 2 they received that initial deposit of treasure on the day of Pentecost, *"and they were all filled with the Holy Spirit ..." (verse 4).*

They went about distributing this. They preached to the masses, and three thousand received that power and were born again. They raised a cripple, preached again to the chief priests and elders, all the time releasing that treasure of power.

They returned to their prayer closets empty, and prayed for more. We are told in Acts 4:31 that: *"They were all filled with the Holy Spirit, and they spoke the word of God with boldness."*

What had happened? They had been refilled and empowered for further service.

As we give out God's treasury in preaching, healing and casting out demons like the early disciples, our power treasury drops its level. If we wish to continue in boldness and power our treasury reserves have to be kept at a high level.

There are a few ways this can be achieved:

1. Like the disciples, we can pray for boldness and power;

2. In Ephesians 5:18-19 we are told: *"But be filled with the Spirit, speaking to one another in psalms and hymns and spiritual songs, making melody in your heart to the Lord;* and

3. Jude 20 says: *"But you beloved, building yourselves up on your most holy faith praying in the Holy Spirit.*

This praying in the Holy Spirit is confirmed in 1

Corinthians 14:4: *"He who speaks in an unknown tongue edifies himself"*

"Edify" means "to build yourself up," as mentioned in Jude 20.

Speaking in tongues is the spiritual excercise I do before going out to do any ministry. If I am going to rely on the Holy Spirit power, I must be full of that power.

This is a basic ingredient that many fail to apply. They know the power is needed, but will not put in the necessary time to build themselves up. The result is a flop.

The apostle Paul realised what was needed to keep his treasury of power going and said in 1 Corinthians 14:18: *"I thank God I speak in tongues more than you all."*

Spend as much time as you can singing psalms, hymns and spiritual songs, and most importantly, speaking in tongues.

This will ensure that you are always filled with the power of the Holy Spirit, and ready to release the Holy Spirit treasury of power to those in need.

If you would like to be released in your heavenly language pray this prayer aloud.

"Father God, in the Name of Jesus Christ and the power of the Holy Spirit release me in my personal prayer language right now.

Bind and break any bondage in my mind which will hinder me.

As I in faith release sound and allow the Holy Spirit to guide my mouth and my tongue, Your language will be released. In faith I begin to speak right now."

Chapter 10

YOUR BADGE OF AUTHORITY

We now move on to the next ingredient in our recipe. When Peter prayed for the paralytic, he used the name of Jesus Christ of Nazareth.

"Silver and gold I do not have but what I do have I give you: IN THE NAME OF JESUS CHRIST OF NAZARETH rise up and walk." (Acts 3:6).

The name of Jesus Christ is an ingredient which cannot be left out, if we are going to witness the sick healed. We are told more than once in Scripture about this important key.

He tells us: *"If you ask anything in My name, I will do it."* (John 14:14).

Many of us have failed to receive promises from God because we have not prayed in the name of Jesus Christ.

We may have missed blessings from our prayers because of our lack of knowledge. In future we should determine to use the name all the time. *"And whatever you do in word or deed, DO ALL IN THE NAME OF THE LORD JESUS, giving thanks to God the Father through Him."* (Colossians 3:17).

Not Just the Name

I've heard many Christians say: "Well I've prayed in Jesus' name and nothing happened!"

The name of Jesus Christ is not some word that works like magic when you use it.

When Peter was talking about the lame man who was healed, he said: *"... His Name, through faith in His Name has made this man strong."*

J.B. Phillips translates it: *"...It is faith in that Name, which has cured this man..."*

Notice it was not just the name of Jesus. It was FAITH IN THE NAME that healed him.

Without faith in the name you may run into trouble, just as the seven sons of Sceva did in Acts 19:13-16. They had been watching Paul deliver people from demons and noted that he kept using the name of Jesus Christ.

"Ah!" they must have thought to themselves, "We've got the magic word. Just use the name of Jesus and demons will leave!" They approached a demon possessed person and said: "We adjure you by the Jesus that Paul preaches."

The demon answered and said: "Jesus I know, Paul I know, but who are you?" The demon beat them up badly, stripped them and they ran for their lives.

Now we don't want you to end up second best as those men did. Therefore, this section is not just designed to teach you to use the Name, but to build faith in the Name. You then will have the same excitement and success that the original disciples had.

"The seventy returned with joy, saying: 'Lord, even the demons are subject to us IN YOUR NAME.'" (Luke 10:17).

Jesus' Authority

Why is there authority in this Name?

"Therefore God also has highly exalted Him and given Him the name which is above every name, that at the name of Jesus every knee should bow, of those in heaven and of those on earth and of those under the earth." (Philippians 2:9,10).

It is a Name with more power than any president, king or queen or any other person on earth Jesus declared that: *"... All authority has been given to Me in heaven and on earth." (Matthew 28:18).*

Our Authority

Jesus handed the authority of His Name to all believers, to enable them to do the works that He did. He said: *"...IN MY NAME they will cast out demons ... they will lay hands on the sick, and they will recover." (Mark 16:17,18).*

Through faith in His name we have the ability to release the power of God that's in us.

How Does It Work?

One of the purposes of being a president or leader of a country is to keep law and order. However the leader cannot go around arresting every criminal himself. Jesus came to this earth for the purpose of rendering powerless the works of the devil (1 John 3:8). Like any other leader, He could not possibly go around arresting every work of the devil himself.

A president delegates a police force who, with their badges of authority, arrest people IN THE NAME OF THE LAW.

Our leader has delegated us as His spiritual police

110

force, and give us a badge of authority so we can arrest the devil's works **IN THE NAME OF JESUS CHRIST**.

When a person joins the police force, he swears an oath of allegiance to the State to uphold the law of the land. He is then given the badge which gives him the power and authority to arrest evil doers. The badge comes with the job.

When you joined Jesus' force, you declared allegiance to Him and declared through His power to follow His laws. You are given a badge of authority to arrest any work of the enemy.

"Behold, I give you the authority to trample on serpents and scorpions, and over all the power of the enemy, and nothing shall by any means hurt you." (Luke 10:19).

You don't earn the badge. It comes automatically to enable you to do your job.

Imagine if I was a plain clothes policeman and I went up to a criminal and simply said: "I arrest you!"

He is quite within his rights to resist me. He could say: "Who do you think you are?" However, if I then showed him my police badge, what would his attitude be? I'm sure he would change: "Oh, I'm sorry sir, I didn't realise who you were. I'll go anywhere you tell me."

Many Christians have tried to cast out demons in their own strength.

"I cast you out!" I've heard them emphasize, giving no importance to the Name of Jesus.

Many of these wonder why nothing happened. Like the criminal, the demon could say "Who do you think you are?" (As they did to the sons of Sceva). We are to show them whose power and authority we are operating under by showing them our badge. "In the Name of Jesus Christ, I arrest your power!" brings a different response.

"Yes Sir, I didn't realise who you were, I'll go anywhere you tell me."

It wouldn't matter if I was a huge policeman or a small one. The criminal is not afraid of the size of the person, they are only afraid of the badge he carries. The smallest policeman carries exactly the same authority to arrest as the biggest.

When you carry your spiritual badge, it doesn't matter if you are tall, short, fat, thin, male, female, soft voice or loud voice. It has nothing to do with your physical qualities but everything to do with your badge and your faith in it.

"IN MY NAME, you shall cast out demons."

Amazing Results - A Testimony

Once we grasp the truth in this authority, knees will bow to the Name of Jesus Christ. This story is the testimony of a young lady called Cecily Stoneham, one of our associates at International Outreach:

"Earlier this year, while travelling in New South Wales, I was teaching a seminar in a Church of about 200 people. On the third night, I had really been sensing that God was going to do something new and exciting, but had no idea what lay ahead.

"This particular night the teaching was on the principle of authority in the Name of Jesus Christ. I was almost through the second session, when a woman, whom we later found out to be a witch, crashed through the back doors and disrupted the meeting. Fear gripped the congregation and the hair on the back of my neck stood up. The woman came down the aisle towards me so dramatically that I thought she was going to pull a knife on me. I was petrified, silently crying out to God for help.

"Now eyeball to eyeball, she spat in my face. I was almost relieved that was all she did. I asked the Lord what to do next, and I said to her: 'Please sit down and wait until the end of the meeting.'

"She flatly refused.

"Not knowing exactly how to reply, I realised that the next step was to use my authority in the Name of Jesus.

"That's what I did.

"The power of God hit her and sent her sprawling on the floor.

"The Name of Jesus Christ is effective.

"I then realised I still had another 15 minutes left to preach and was concerned she may get up and cause further disruption. I said to her: 'In the name of Jesus Christ, stay there till the end of the meeting.'

"That was exactly what happened!

"Along with the congregation, I was seeing the principle of the Name in action, and obviously God wanted it demonstrated that night. Gradually the congregation relaxed and some even began giggling in excitement.

"Later, we witnessed to that woman, and she told us that she had tried to get up several times during the meeting, but couldn't. God was faithful to His Word. She received Christ as her Saviour and was set free by the power of God."

Only the Name Of Jesus? - Stuart's Story

"During an evangelistic meeting, I was moving along a healing line, praying. Suddenly a girl from the line ran backwards, snarling and hissing at me, waving her arms with karate type threatenings. Not wishing to give the enemy any margin I commanded: 'You come here in Jesus' Name!'

"You come here in MY Jesus' name!" she snapped back devilishly.

"I was stunned; surely under this evil influence she shouldn't use the Name of Jesus!

"We found out later that this girl had seriously been seeking the Lord, but she was still not totally delivered and Satan still had control over her in certain areas.

"We later talked, and she told me some of her past. She had been a witch, the head of a coven, and had actually "married" Satan. He manifested as a man and called himself 'Jesus'.

"She had married a 'Jesus'. When she was saying: 'Come here in MY Jesus' name', she was referring to the devil. She told us that someone like her, who had been possessed by a very powerful spirit, would need to have the Name of Jesus Christ used.

"I was a little skeptical of this advice, however I thought I would check in the Bible to either disprove or confirm her claim. Although the Scriptures do say that at the Name of Jesus every knee shall bow, I found that in cases of deliverance or sickness or demons, that the full Name of Jesus Christ was used.

"Paul delivered a woman from a spirit of divination:

"...Paul, being grieved said...I command you in the name of JESUS CHRIST to come out of her." (Acts 16:18).

"Peter raised the paralytic Aeneas who had been bedridden for eight years:

"...JESUS the CHRIST heals you. Arise and make your bed. Then he arose immediately." (Acts 9:34).

"Again, when Peter raised that cripple at the Gate Beautiful:

"Silver and gold I do not have, but what I do have I give you: In the name of JESUS CHRIST OF NAZARETH rise up and walk." (Acts 3:6).

"Peter even nominated where he came from. There was going to be no confusion as to which Jesus he meant!

"Why did they use the Name JESUS CHRIST and not just Jesus?

"Throughout history many people have used the Name of Jesus. Even in the time of Jesus there were others called by that Name.

"'Christ' however means 'the anointed one'. Not just any Jesus, but the one anointed by the Holy Ghost and power.

"Remember, we said earlier, it is faith in the Name that is needed.

"I have found after that experience a new revelation of His might and power have flowed through me.

"Using that full title "Jesus Christ" is a constant reminder to me of who He is and what authority I have. It helps me have faith in the Name.

"Perhaps like me you only used the Name of Jesus in the past. Now, just as Peter and Paul did, I use that full

Name as a constant reminder that I represent, and am an enforcer for, the most powerful and anointed Name on the earth today."

Demons Fear the Name

On the cross of Calvary a complete defeat of Satan and his forces was witnessed.

"Having disarmed principalities and powers, He made a public spectacle of them, triumphing over them in it." *(Colossians 2:15).*

Just imagine spending a round of boxing with the heavy weight champion of the world, and receiving the greatest beating of your life. You would be scared to death to face him in the next round. At the end of round one, he leaves the ring. You breathe a sigh of relief, then he walks around and says to you: "My younger brother is going to fight you in the next round. If you think I fight well, the same beating that I gave you, he will give also, in fact, it will be even greater!" That would really make you feel great, wouldn't it?

That first round with Jesus at Calvary completely put the devil down and rendered him powerless.

Jesus Christ has put the boxing gloves on His younger brother, the Church, and said: "The works that I do he will do also, and greater works than these he will do." He wants us to go out into the world and destroy the works of the enemy as He did, it's our fight now till the final bell."

We have a knock-out punch in the Name of Jesus Christ. Use it and you will have the devil on the canvas!

We have three reasons why the fight is not being won today. We have one group of fighters who have their gloves on, but are too nervous to come out and use what they have.

We have another group who had courage to begin fighting, but because they didn't have all the skills needed to win, they lost the first couple of rounds. Then they went to the neutral corner and refuse to come out again. They claim they have no "ministry" of boxing.

Thirdly, we have the majority who have not even ventured into the ring. They are cheering and believing for the pastors and evangelists to go and knock out the devil, unaware they are supposed to be fighters too!

REALISE THAT WE ALL HAVE TO FIGHT THE DEVIL. There may come an attack on your family. In your daily walk, there will be people with needs. It is not always possible to send them to the pastor. If you are there, God will expect you to put on those gloves and win. This is not just some game you will be fighting. The prize is the health of those people.

Learn to arm yourself now, so that when you are confronted by a person who is afflicted, you will know that you have the victory.

Chapter 11

YOU ARE A COMMANDER

Our third ingredient in our recipe of Acts 3:6 is that of commanding:

"...But what I do have I give you: In the name of Jesus Christ of Nazareth, rise up and walk." (Acts 3:6).

Not only did Peter use the Name of Jesus Christ, and not only did he release the power. He also commanded: "Rise up and walk!"

The Godhead Commands

Where does this principle of commanding come from? We are told: *"...The worlds were framed by the word of God..."* (Hebrews 11:3). *"Then God said, Let there be light, and there was light." (Genesis 1:3).*

God commanded the universe into existence. Jesus used the principle of commanding also in John 11:43. He commanded the dead Lazarus: *"Come forth"*. He also commanded a storm to cease, *"Peace, be still." (Mark 4:39).*

We are to Command

We are told that we are made in the image of God (Genesis 1:26) and are to be conformed *"to the image of His Son." (Romans 8:29).* Obviously, as His children, we are to do as He does. We are told to be "followers". This word in the original Greek means to mimic or imitate. We are to *"be 'imitators' of God as dear children." (Ephesians 5:1).*

After all, as I heard one preacher say: "Children of the devil act like the devil. So children of God should act like God."

As a young boy I used to get in our family car, and with all the appropriate noises, "drive" the car like dad. My sister constantly dressed up in my mother's old clothes, and stumbled around the house in high heel shoes. It was natural for us to mimic our parents. Jesus did what He saw His Father do (John 5:19). Our Heavenly Father expects the same of us. He sent His son Jesus Christ as our Example, and we are to conduct ourselves on earth as He did.

Jesus Christ set people free by commanding healings. Let us follow that Example as good children should.

Commanders in Christ

God declares that we, His children, are priests and kings (Revelation 1:6). A king commands or decrees things. *"You will also declare a thing, and it will be established for you:..."(Job 22:28).*

For years in India, we have been conducting large city wide "JESUS HEALS" campaigns. These involve team members from the United Kingdom, Australia and New Zealand, and have resulted in the Gospel being preached, with signs and wonders following, to more than two million people.

Our crusade teams of around fifty "training" saints preach throughout the city in slums, streets and market places, and each night they pray for the tens of thousands that come for healing prayer.

They "TAKE THE CITY" in the same way that Philip

took Samaria. It is like reliving the Book of Acts, as miracles and healings flow.

During one of these campaigns, tens of thousands had made decisions for the Lord. Word of the healings had spread everywhere, and like Samaria, there was great joy in the city.

Then the enemy moved!

The weather bureau forecast that a cyclone, which was out to sea, would cross the coast over the town in which we were preaching. We were into the final crusade nights and huge crowds were expected. The ground in which we were preaching was very low, and past experience had shown that even light rain would convert it to mud. As most of the people attending the meetings sat on the ground, rain would mean cancellation! The crusade team prayed that the cyclone would completely miss the city. We then walked around the ground and commanded it to "STAY DRY! BONE DRY!"

The cyclone completely circled the city, and all surrounding villages in which we had preached a few days earlier experienced minor flooding. Our prayers were answered. The cyclone did not touch the city itself, and word went around even among the Hindus, that the cyclone had not touched the city because of the Christians' presence.

We praised God, but to our utter disappointment very light rain fell intermittently all day, and I knew it was enough to ruin the ground for the final two nights. Around 5p.m, a couple of hours before our campaign was due to start, the rain finally stopped. I joined our co-ordinator to see the extent of the damage to the ground and whether alternative seating arrangements could be made.

Climbing onto the dais, we noticed that rain water had collected on the tent, covering the platform area. As we stepped down onto the ground we were amazed to find how dry it was. I stamped my foot and dust rose up. It was bone dry! Quite honestly, I was just as surprised as the local men. The rain had fallen on the stage area and around the outskirts of the ground- but not ON it!

The campaign went ahead with great success. I had learned a practical lesson in the power of commanding.

We have continually used the principle to set the deaf, dumb, lepers, lame and many others free.

"...Whoever says to this mountain, 'be removed and be cast into the sea' and does not doubt in his heart, but believes that those things he says will come to pass, he will have whatever he says." (Mark 11:23).

We can speak to mountains of sickness and diseases in people's bodies and set them free.

Speak With Authority

As a king, you must speak like a king. Can you imagine a king whispering or making suggestions to a person subject to him? You need to communicate firmly and clearly so that there is no mistaking what your decree is.

When Jesus raised Lazarus, it was a strong clear command.

"He cried with a loud voice, 'Lazarus come forth'!" (John 11:43).

Paul was an imitator of Jesus. He commanded a

paralytic man to rise. Paul said with a loud voice, "Stand upright on your feet!"

Notice, that in both cases it was with a "loud" voice.

Sometimes we need to use the "ingredient" of commanding in a loud voice.

This does not mean screaming or yelling.

I've seen parents who have no authority over their children. The child runs away, the mother screaming out: "Johnny! ... come back here!"

The child takes no notice and runs even faster.

I've seen Christians dealing with demonic activity and making a lot of noise with no results.

But you parents who have authority also realise that when your child misbehaves really badly, and you correct them, the tone of your voice rises. An authority comes into your voice. The child immediately knows that he is in trouble and has to obey.

We have total authority through the Name of Jesus Christ. When we command demons or sickness to go, that same authority should show up in the tone of your voice, just as it did with Jesus and Paul.

This authoritive loud voice lets demons realise you know who you are and whose authority you are operating under. They, as your children would do, obey your command.

Won't a Quiet Prayer Do?

Oh, I have wished on many occasions that a quiet prayer would be enough to heal! I have ministered in conservative churches where people are not used to healing services and the principle of commanding. It would be so much "nicer" if we did not have to be loud at times. In my earlier ministry at one particular church, I asked the Lord: "Can't we have it nice and quiet today please Jesus? I want them to embrace this healing message and perhaps commanding could upset them."

After preaching and calling for the sick to come forward, the first man to come out had a pain in his lower back. Naturally, wanting to raise faith in the other people, I was believing for him to be healed instantly. I prayed a beautiful soft prayer. I am sure all the congregation were suitably impressed. "He is not some radical," they would probably have thought. "He obviously has a lot of love in him!" I stood back rather saintly and asked how he was. "Nothing happened," he shot back at me. I prayed another equally nice prayer, then another. Still nothing happened.

I could feel the faith of the congregation falling through the floor.

What was I to do? I suppose I could have said: "God is healing you, and you will get better, sometime."

I knew however, that this particular congregation would be thinking: "It can't be God's will to heal him at all," as they knew little about divine healing. I screamed from my mind: "What's going wrong Lord?"

The Lord said to me: "Do you want him healed or do you want to keep up those nice prayers?"

"I want him healed!" I said, somewhat taken back.

"Then command it!"

"Spirit of infirmity," I cried in a loud voice, "come out of him, in the Name of Jesus Christ!"

I am sure everyone jumped up twelve inches from their

pews, but by the time they had landed, the man was instantly healed and we continued to see many MORE MIRACLES.

India Experience

I was watching some video shots of our crusades and noticed a shot of myself praying for a beautiful little deaf girl. It was late and we had prayed for hundreds and I was very tired. I prayed for that ear quietly and then looked back at a very disappointed and disillusioned face.

I became angry and shouted: "Come out of her!" Immediately her face changed. She could hear and a broad smile broke out across her face. Seeing that video simply re-emphasized the importance of commanding.

The ingredient of commanding is not used every time, as we will explain more fully later.

However, if we don't use it when needed, it can be that we leave a person disappointed instead of bringing happiness and joy.

Chapter 12

A MAN OF ACTION

As a former businessman, I only too well remembered being taught many principles in the "school of hard knocks!" One important principle I learned was through a business convention, dealing with "ingredients for success".

In the conference room, just after breakfast, the visiting speaker began in a very unusual way.

"Everyone get off your chairs and look under them!"

We all obeyed in child-like manner. Can you picture it? About fifty immaculately dressed businessmen each finding a dollar note fastened under their chairs!

"Take that dollar note and sit down again," was his command. Everyone obeyed.

Ingredient number one in a successful business," he lectured, "If you want to make a buck, you've got to get off your seat!"

Everyone enjoyed the joke, but I have never forgotten the principle. As we will see, action is a very important part of seeing healing take place.

The Saints In Action

This final ingredient in our story of the cripple in Acts 3 shows action to be a vital part in seeing the man healed. *"In the name of Jesus Christ of Nazareth, rise up and walk. And he took him by the right hand, and LIFTED HIM UP; and immediately his feet and ankle bones received strength."*

(verses 6 and 7).

Only after lifting him up, did his feet and ankle bones receive strength. Action is apparent in so many of the recorded healings. We also see FAITH IN ACTION before and during healings.

In Luke 6:8-10 the story of the healing of the man with the withered hand shows that Jesus requested that he stand up in front of everyone in the synagogue on the Sabbath.

Anyone aligning themselves to Jesus was put out of the synagogue. (John 9:22).

Now, here was Jesus telling this man to stand up. Every eye would have been on him. I can imagine the thoughts of his friends - one perhaps tugging at his coat and saying softly: "Sit down you idiot, do you want to get into trouble?" But he arose in faith, in obedience to what Jesus had requested, and then after he had done his part Jesus was able to do the rest.

"Stretch out your hand." His hand was restored!

We are all familiar with the story in John 9:1-8, where Jesus made clay for a blind man and put it in his eyes. By faith that man received his healing, by acting out what Jesus told him to do.

"Go, wash in the pool of SILOAM."

We see many faith actions in the Bible of varying degrees. There were times when Jesus acted. Other times it was the person.

"If I may touch His garment I shall be made whole," said the woman with an issue of blood. She touched Him and was healed.

Faith in action was also demonstrated in Mark 2:3-5,

where a paralytic was carried by four men to the house where Jesus was.

They couldn't get through the huge crowd, so they went onto the roof, broke it open and lowered the paralytic down to Jesus.

The Bible says: "When Jesus saw their faith."

How can you "see" faith. Firstly, the faith of the paralytic, telling the men to carry him up and tear open the roof. Secondly, their faith in actually doing it.

Jesus answered that "action" faith and healed him.

Action faith can either be used by the person praying, the person receiving or both combined.

Let's talk about both types, and the need for both.

Your Faith in Action.

In many cases, it is the operation of your FAITH IN ACTION, that is the final ingredient in seeing someone healed.

In the case of Peter with the cripple, HE took the cripple and lifted him up.

If Peter had not used the final ingredient, and pulled the beggar to his feet he might have sat begging for the rest of his life. That night he might have said to some other beggars: "Boy, what a day! I was just sitting there, when suddenly some maniac came at me and started screaming about not having any silver and gold, and about someone called Jesus.

"And then to top it off, he told me I could walk!"

No, Peter used the final ingredient of lifting him, and the man was healed.

Why did it work? I believe the power of God was

working already in the man's body. He could not see it, feel it, or know it was there.

By Peter lifting him, it showed the man that he was healed.

India Experience

One day, I was called to pray for an old Indian pastor who was apparently dying. He had not eaten or had anything to drink for four days, due to a blockage in his throat.

I arrived to the sound of wailing friends and parishioners who were all expecting him to die. I prayed for him, and immediately he felt his throat clear and thanked me for my prayers. I left contented I had done all I could.

Two days later, on the Sunday, his son came and requested my prayers again. "He has not moved from his bed, his throat has closed up again, and he has now not eaten or drunk for six days." Realizing I must have missed it somewhere, I went down again, to the accompaniment of all the wailing and crying, and I commanded all the unbelievers out of the room!

With only the family present I again commanded that lump to disappear, and cried out: "Get out of that bed in the name of Jesus Christ." I grabbed him by the hand and pulled him out of bed. The relatives were shocked and the old man stood there shaking and stunned.

"Get some milk and food," I ordered.

When they arrived I told him to eat and drink. He looked at me very unsure.

"Eat" I said.

He ate and drank, got himself cleaned up and was in church praising God within the hour.

I met that pastor four years later. He was still ministering, and admitted that if he hadn't acted on his faith, his throat would have once again closed up, and he would have died.

Their Faith In Action

When you pray for somebody, quite often they don't feel God's power go in, and they are still unsure. They need to be stirred into action to show them that something has happened.

If people are using such items as crutches, walking sticks, glasses, hearing aids, get them to put them aside and try to operate without them.

Be very wise in this area - some people may be recovering. For example, a person with a walking stick may need your assistance for the first few steps as reassurance.

If there are problems with aches or pains, get them to move the affected area and check themselves, so they know immediately if something happened. Even if the pain is reduced a little, it gives them the confidence that God has started his work and they shall recover.

One time, in India, we preached on this message of Acts 3, and Peter's miracle. I had instructed all the polio and lame to be brought to the front of the stage prior to the meeting. After preaching we simply told the people to stand up just as that crippled man had.

People stood everywhere. A mother put her former polio affected child on the stage, and saw it run back and forth for the first time!

*"Look at the excited expressions on the team members faces,
as this former polio afflicted girl walks for the first time."*

Chapter 13

GETTING STARTED PRAYER 1

We have now covered many ingredients of healing prayer.

1. Preaching the Gospel;
2. Laying hands on the sick;
3. Allowing recovery time;
4. Realisation of the Holy Spirit power within us;
5. Using the Name of Jesus Christ;
6. Commanding;
7. Using Action.

We are going to combine these ingredients and give you recipes for two basic prayers that will enable you to begin praying for the sick.

We mention TWO basic prayers, because we found through the Scriptures and by experience, that sickness and physical afflictions originate from two entirely different sources:

1. DIRECT DEMON AFFLICTION; and
2. PHYSICAL IMPAIRMENT.

Demonic Affliction

There are many cases recorded in the Bible where sickness was the direct result of demons, devils or spirits. People were healed in each case as the spirit was cast off.

Many Christians, even today, still have difficulty with

the concept of demons or evil spirits. Many of us have learned to believe modern medicine more than we believe the Bible.

Medical science has a lot of catching up to do with the incredible teaching in God's Word.

In the nineteenth century, doctors scoffed at the idea of bacteria. They didn't exist because they couldn't see them. They did not wash their hands or instruments before surgery, bacteria spread, and many people died as a result.

It took many centuries for modern medicine to catch up with the basic sanitary instructions of hand washing and cleansing which were given way back in Moses' day.

Medical science is still centuries behind in the area of the spirit realm. Many today scoff at the idea of spirits because like their nineteenth century counterparts, they can't see them.

Because of this non acceptance, many doctors, as well meaning and compassionate as they are, only treat the symptoms with pain killers, and are unable to get to the cause.

However, many progressive Christian doctors, who have seen the reality of this nearly two-thousand-year old teaching are now praying for those who were previously "incurable" or had "recurring problems", and seeing good results.

We today also must realise that Jesus knows more about healing bodies than anybody. If we are going to be able to heal "all" as He did, we must also diagnose and pray as He did. Let's go through a few cases that would be presumed incurable today, and see how Jesus dealt with them.

DUMB: *"...they brought to Him (Jesus) a man, mute and DEMON- POSSESSED. And when the demon was cast out, the mute spoke..." (Matthew 9:32,33).*

When many of us hear the word "possessed," we can think it means the person is a maniac, completely out of control.

This of course can be the case, where a spirit can possess the person's entire mind and then speak and move through them.

In this case it is only minor possession. The spirit is possessing or controlling the vocal chords.

If someone came up to you and grabbed you by the throat, you would be unable to speak. They are possessing or controlling your vocal chords. If another person cast them off you, then you would be released and be free to talk again.

This is what had happened to this man. His voice was controlled by the spirit causing him to be dumb. Jesus cast it off, and he was then able to speak.

BAD BACKS

Jesus dealt with an extremely bad back condition in Luke 13:11,12: *"...There was a woman who had a SPIRIT OF INFIRMITY eighteen years, and was bent over ... Jesus said to her, 'Woman, you are loosed from your infirmity.'"*

This woman had been bent over for eighteen years. If she had gone to the doctor today, he may have called it arthritis. Jesus attributed the problem to the devil, and called it a "spirit of infirmity".

At a town called Samalkot, a woman approached us, whose back was permanently bent at a 90 degree angle and so she constantly looked at the ground. I laid my hands on her and cast out a spirit of infirmity. Slowly she began to stand up, straighter and straighter. After about a minute she stood perfectly tall, raised her hands and praised God excitedly. We found out later why she was so jubilant. She had been in that position for twelve years!

We then preached the Gospel to those who witnessed that healing on the roadside, and over 80 village people made commitments to Christ.

A Personal Experience:

This realm became very much alive to me on a ministry trip to Auckland in New Zealand. A woman, complaining of continuous pain for some weeks in her lower back, came out for prayer. As I laid hands on her, I received a word from the Lord, who told me that the problem was a spirit.

I commanded it to leave and immediately she cried out: "The pain has moved". Pain does not normally move after being in one place for three weeks. At the same time, the Lord opened up my spiritual eyes and I saw this demon rush up her back and attach itself just below the back of her neck.

I was so shocked. Without thinking, I called out: "You rotten little thing - get off!"

You won't find that prayer in the Gospels ...but it worked!

The woman fell flat on the floor as the spirit left. After a few moments she regained her feet, and was totally healed.

To this day, that is the only time I have observed a spirit in healing ministry.

The Lord, I believe, was showing me the reality of this usually "unseen" enemy. Knowing that reality of these spirits has helped me untold times in dealing with many problems that doctors simply could not heal.

Countless numbers, who have been on pain killers for aches, pains, stiff joints and arthritic conditions, have been easily healed as we have commanded these spirits to leave.

DEAF AND DUMB

The problem of deafness and dumbness can also originate from spirits.

"...He (Jesus) rebuked the unclean spirit, saying to him, 'You DEAF AND DUMB SPIRIT, I command you, come out of him..." (Mark 9:25).

After removing dumb spirits, we have found in some cases particularly with children, another problem - they try to imitate your words but no sound comes out.

They haven't ever used their voice box, and don't know how. We found by putting their hands on our vocal chords, and then speaking, they realized where the sound needed to come from. Within a minute, they would then be able to imitate this and speak perfectly.

EPILEPSY AND MENTAL ILLNESS:

"Lord, have mercy on my son, for he is an epileptic and suffers severely; for he often falls into the fire...And Jesus

rebuked the demon, and he came out of him…" (Matthew 17:15 and 18).

A spirit can attack the brain causing such complaints as epilepsy and forms of mental illness. However, we are not saying all mental illness comes from spirits.

At one meeting a girl of about 16 was brought to us by her parents. Her eyes were wandering and she was obviously demented. Her parents pointed to her head and explained that she was insane. After prayer, she was thrown backwards on the floor, similarly to the boy in Mark 9:26, "as one dead". Twenty minutes later she awoke, clear eyed and sane, set free completely from that demon spirit.

BLINDNESS

"Then one was brought to Him who was DEMON-POSSESSED, blind and mute, and He healed him…" (Matthew 12:22).

We have noted many blind, whose eyes appear perfect with no apparent physical defect. After commanding the spirit of blindness to leave, immediately they could see.

Between the eye and the brain runs the optic nerve which transmits the "pictures". My personal belief is that the spirit possesses this nerve. Once the spirit is cast off, the nerve can carry out its intended function and sight is restored.

FEAR

An evangelist friend of mine dealt with a boy who was dumb and through a Word of Knowledge was told a spirit of fear bound the boy. He cast it out and immediately the boy could talk perfectly. We have found this same spirit, in some instances, to be the cause of stuttering.

In New Zealand a teenager was bought to our meetings who could not walk without the help of two big metal walking sticks. As I went to pray for him, I felt led to ask when it had happened. As a youngster learning to walk, he had had a bad fall, and had been unable to walk properly from that time. I cast out a spirit of fear.

He was very careful at first, trying to walk without the sticks, and so I helped him. Within a few minutes, he was able to move without any assistance, and he walked out with his friend who now had the sticks tucked under his arm.

Your Prayer for Spirits

To get you started, we have three basic steps for your prayer.

Ingredient No. 1 - Speak to the Mountain:

Mark 11:23 says: *"If you say to the mountain to be removed, ...you shall have whatever you say."* This is the principle of commanding. You simply name the mountain of sickness or problem.

I've come across Christians who get themselves into considerable difficulties in dealing with demons. "You must know the name of the demon," I've heard some say, "otherwise it can't come out!"

They then feel if the spirit doesn't tell them it's name or unless they get a Word of Knowledge they can't pray for the person.

Now certainly there are times when the Lord reveals

the problem through a Word of Knowledge or another spiritual gift, but I have found that most of the time it doesn't seem to work that way.

If we want to know the names of spirits in the physical realm, Jesus shows us very simply how to do it.

When he came up to someone who was deaf, he called the spirit a "deaf spirit".

When he came up to someone who was infirmed, he called the spirit a "spirit of infirmity".

When he came up to someone who was blind, he called the spirit a "blind spirit".

If you are not sure what the problem is, for instance, a pain in a woman's stomach, you simply say: "You spirit that's causing the pain."

They know you are talking to them.

Let's not over complicate something that was meant to be so simple.

Ingredient No. 2 - Binding and Loosing:

The Scripture tells us, *"...and whatever you bind on earth will be bound in heaven, and whatever you loose on earth will be loosed in heaven." (Matthew 16:19).*

To "bind" means "to tie up or constrain". To "loose" means "to release". You, with your command, bind (constrain) the power of the enemy and then you loose it (release it from the person being prayed for).

Jesus said to the woman with the spirit of infirmity: *"Woman, you are loosed from your infirmity." (Luke 13:11, 12).*

Ingredient No. 3 - In My Name:

"In My Name you shall cast out demons."

We use the badge of authority, the name of Jesus

Christ, as we learnt previously.

We simply now combine all three ingredients:

1. Name the problem;
2. Bind and loosen it's power,
3. Use your authority in His name.

Example:

1. "Spirit of Deafness" (or simply "deafness")
2. "I bind your power over this person.
3. "Loosen them and set them free, right now, in the Name of Jesus Christ."

Learn these prayer ingredients by heart. When you are praying for someone you need to be relaxed and thinking of your authority in Jesus. You don't want to be digging through your notes and asking "Now, how did that prayer go again?"

Different Strengths

In the spirit realm, demons have varying levels of power. Our experience has been that deaf, dumb and spirits of infirmity are some of the weaker spirits and they can be removed even by those just beginning to pray for the sick.

Sometimes the healing a deaf or dumb person can seem above our faith levels. Remember, you are only dealing with a weak little spirit, and they are great starting places which can boost you on to greater works in God.

Compassionate Anger

Another ingredient that will help you to increase your authority, is that of love. Jesus loved people so much, he

139

could not stand to see sickness stay on their bodies.

Imagine a young bride who, with her mother has spent months choosing materials, designing and preparing a wedding gown. On the wedding day, she walks to the bridal car with her mother in close attendance. Just as she nears the road, another vehicle flashes by, mud flies through the air and lands on her dress.

What is the reaction of the mother?

She is totally upset, and repulsed by the incident. She rushes in to remove that mud. She will do all in her power to make sure that the mess is removed. Why? She loves her daughter and knows the effect the mud will have on her.

Christians are the Bride of Christ. When we see sickness or spirits on a person's body, it is like mud on that bride's dress.

Jesus wants Christians to be a Bride "without spot or blemish." The same repulsion the bride's mother would feel should arise in us. With compassionate anger, we should rise against the devil's works that are hurting others.

This righteous anger will automatically bring a fervour, an authority, which will help us command demons to leave.

Remember Commanding

The Scriptures tell us: *"You shall cast out demons."* This does not mean a nice polite request. "Cast" means to "drive out by force." Remember my failure to heal the man's back in that church where I prayed so beautifully and quietly? I was dealing with a spirit. You can't say:

"Please, Mr. spirit will you leave?"

Look at our example with Jesus *"...You deaf and dumb spirit, I command you, come out of him..." (Mark 9:25).*

Imagine a crazy little dog chewing and attacking the leg of a man's trousers. What do you think the effect would be if he said: "Nice doggie, please let go of my trousers, as you may tear them."

That would probably encourage the dog to continue.

His next request would become a little louder: "Please let me go!"

Still no results.

Finally, he becomes so annoyed and desperate he yells out and stamps his foot on the ground: "Get out of here you mutt!"

The dog, now terrified, runs for its life. TREAT DEMONS LIKE CRAZY LITTLE DOGS...COMMAND THEM!

Exercise

Total authority is given to you as a believer to carry out ministry.

"These signs shall follow those who believe...they shall cast out demons in My name."

You are a believer!

You can cast out demons!

You can do the works that Jesus did!

Write your name in the space provided and repeat the Scripture again:

"These signs shall follow _____
who believes... _____ *shall cast out demons in My Name,"* (see Mark 16:17).

141

Repeat this three or four times and picture yourself doing the works that Jesus and countless other Christians before you have done.

_____ can cast out deafness.

_____ can cast out dumbness.

_____ can cast out infirmities.

Evil spirits know those who have learnt to have authority in the name of Jesus.

"Jesus I know, Paul I know." (Acts 19:15).

They will know your name as well, as you begin to release this new found authority.

DR. M. BALESTRIERI

MALENY, AUSTRALIA

Graduate of the University of Queensland

Not only have I witnessed the healing power of God time after time, but the reality of the miraculous has now nestled into my consciousness and rocked my former preconceived clinical opinions.

Probability and chance lost their power of deception when the seventh cancer sufferer crossed my path and was declared totally fit.

I now believe in a God who cares for our total welfare and is willing to move on our behalf.

Christian doctors, naturally, realise that modern medicine cannot heal everyone. Many of them, because of a heart desire to help others, have begun praying, using the power of Jesus Christ. Here are just a couple of testimonies of a Singapore doctor who has had many people healed through prayer.

Testimonies:

1. A lady around forty years old, a Catholic, suffered from lumbago (backache) associated with pains in her right arm and right leg for over ten years. When she came to the clinic, she was not able to walk into the consultation room without the help from my nurses. On examination, I found she had as coliosis and her limbs were not equal in length. After we prayed for her, the limbs were equal in length, and her spine straightened and the pain disappeared and she was able to walk out of my consultation room without assistance. I must add that the usual medical consultation and ex amination was first done, but the miracle that took place relieved her on the spot. She had been diagnosed as an old case of rheumatoid arthritis with scoliosis.

2. A girl who developed poliomyelitis in her early years, had gone through a series of orthopaedic operations on her legs, both of which were affected. Even after the operations she walked with her right foot in a flexed position, as her right was shorter. The position of her right foot was in a valgus position. While praying for her, the right leg grew to the same length as her left leg and suddenly I found her ankle to be pliable, like plasticine; and I was able to reduce the foot into its proper position. Because of this, she is now able to walk normally.

Dr David Tan Boon Chee
M.B.B.S. (Singapore)

Chapter 14

GETTING STARTED PRAYER 2

In some areas there has been an over-emphasis on demons, to the point where some people believe that ALL sickness or physical affliction is a direct result of spirits.

This is simply not the case, and surely our own common sense should let us realise this.

If I break my arm; it is not a spirit of broken arm.

If I burn my leg; it is not a devil of burnt leg.

If I cut my finger; it is not a demon of cut finger.

Not everyone who is deaf can have the cause directly related to a spirit. Some people are born without an eardrum. A restoration miracle is needed in this case.

A person who is blind, may have had a car accident. Glass, not a spirit, may have damaged the eye.

Physical Impairment

Obviously there are many cases where accidents or afflictions are not the direct result of demon activity.

We will call this category of sickness "PHYSICAL IMPAIRMENT".

Our recipe of Mark 16 gave us two ways of dealing with the sick.

1. "They shall cast out demons;" and
2. "They shall lay hands on the sick."

In our last chapter we dealt with the first of our two

types of prayer. Now we deal with our second - the laying on of hands.

Ingredient No. 1 - Relax:

As mentioned in the chapter on this area, you must realise that you can do nothing by yourself, but: *"I can do all things through Christ who strengthens me." (Philippians 4:13).*

The power inside you is going to do all the work

THIS PRAYER IS COMPLETELY DIFFERENT FROM THE PREVIOUS ONE. THE FORMER PRAYER WAS DEMONSTRATIVE AND LOUD, BECAUSE YOU ARE CASTING SOMETHING OUT.

THIS PRAYER IS GENTLE AND QUIET, BECAUSE YOU ARE SIMPLY ALLOWING THE POWER OF THE HOLY SPIRIT TO FLOW IN TO THEM.

Remember how we likened the Holy Spirit power to electricity.

Picture a big electricity producing power plant that can generate power for thousands of factories and tens of thousands of homes.

Bring that picture to around twelve inches square. Now see that plant inside you. That is still an underrated picture of the Holy Spirit power, but at least you will get the idea.

Your arms are the high voltage lines carrying God's healing power, flowing from the Holy Spirit plant inside you. Imagine it - God's dynamic energy flowing from inside you!

Remember: *"Now to Him who by his power within us is able to do infinitely more than we ever dare to ask or imagine."(Ephesians 3:20 - J.B. Phillips).*

Ingredient No. 2 - Turn on the Power:

If you wish to release electric power in your home, you flick the switch. You can flick the switch of your power source by faith. Simply say: "Holy Spirit, I release Your healing power right now."

Remember now, you are not turning YOURSELF on. You are turning the switch for the Holy Spirit power to flow. You are turning Him on, and switching yourself off. You don't try to do anything - no pentecostal massages - only think of His power flowing out along your arms (high voltage wires) and into the person.

Can you imagine a high voltage wire trying to push electricity along it? No, if you try to do something, you are putting faith in your actions, not in the Holy Spirit.

The result can be that by your negative faith you can limit His power.

Ingredient No. 3 - In the Name of Jesus Christ:

Simply do everything in His Name.

'Be healed and made whole in the Name of Jesus Christ!'

"Made whole" was often used in the prayers of the Gospels.

As we pray, the Holy Spirit power immediately flows in. It reaches the point of need, say the broken arm, and the healing power begins mending it until it recovers.

It flows into the burn and begins to rejuvenate it until it recovers.

It flows into the missing eardrum area and restores an ear drum, making it whole.

Prayer Example

Let's again combine the three ingredients:

"Holy Spirit I release Your healing power right now - be healed and made whole in the Name of Jesus Christ."

Remember, God's power only takes a fraction of a second to flow in. Your prayers need only to be short ones unless you are led otherwise. Again, be sure to learn this by heart, so you can be thinking of His power rather than trying to remember the prayer.

The two prayers we have given you are certainly not the only way to pray, as we will discuss later, but they will give you a Bible-based foundation on which your healing ministry can be launched.

Physical or Spiritual?

With our two prayers available to us, the obvious question may come to our minds: "How do I know which prayer to pray? How do I know if it is a spirit, or simply a physical problem?"

Commonsense will tell you in many cases. In accident areas such as broken bones, cuts, and sprains they are usually physical afflictions. Many people have already been to the doctor before coming to Jesus' power, so use that knowledge to help you discern.

So-called psychosomatic problems are in many cases spirits.

Medical practitioners cannot see the cause, and X-ray machines certainly cannot photograph a spirit. The usual medical treatment prescribed pain killers until "IT" goes away.

We have found many times the "IT" is a spirit, and can be treated by casting it out.

Spiritual Guidance

Sometimes you are faced with a problem that you may not be able to discern. In third world countries we have been confronted with say a dozen deaf and dumb children with no parents to tell us anything. We just lay our hands on each one and ask the Lord. Personally, I have found when I am dealing with a spirit, a small righteous anger rises up within me. If I don't get that anger, I treat it as a physical problem.

For the Beginner

As you may be just beginning to pray for the sick, you may not have your spiritual ear tuned to its fullest capacity as yet. There may be things that you can't discern. For instance, for years I didn't understand what a cold was. Was it spiritual or physical?

In these kind of cases, where you are not sure, do as I did. Pray both prayers.

Use the commanding prayer first. Speak to the mountain. Then release the healing power of God in the second prayer. We have given this prayer a special name. We call it the "DOUBLE WHAMMY". If you don't get the first one to work, the second one will!

Physical and Spiritual Together

There are situations where the two problems can be found together.

Leprosy for instance does not begin as a peeling skin problem.

Neural Leprosy is caused by an internal organism which attacks the nerves. The initial symptoms are no sense of feeling in the arms, hands, feet and sometimes the face. Imagine having two lumps of wood for arms. This is part of the misery that these sufferers face.

As a result of the nerves being "dead", the skin begins to peel away, and mainly through the "wear and tear" of normal living the condition becomes more and more apparent.

When we pray, we work in reverse order. As it was with the cancer, we work first of all with the root. We treat the cause of the problem, the leprosy organism. Using our first prayer, we command the leprosy to go.

In most cases, instantly, feeling is restored to the person. With others it is usually within a few minutes.

For the first time in years they can "feel" their limbs. The excitement from these people is very apparent as they then realise the leprosy is defeated.

Now that the root of the problem is gone, we can pray for the second aspect of the healing and that is for the skin to grow back and be restored.

We complete our prayer and say: "Be healed and made whole in the Name of Jesus Christ."

People on our teams have seen cases where the skin grew back instantly. I prayed for one case where it was restored like new babies' skin within three days.

We have found that in the majority of cases the skin grows back gradually at a normal rate and they recover over a period of weeks.

If a finger or part of a joint is also missing, we need to pray for a recreative miracle, lay our hands on them and simply trust God and command a new joint to be formed.

Other Dual Problems

There are many other cases where the "double whammy" prayer is needed. Like the leprosy, we speak to the root cause, and then allow the healing power to restore physical loss.

Today, people have a great awareness of the power of a virus and the trouble it causes. Polio, for instance, begins through a virus which attacks and weakens parts of the body. We evict the virus first, and then pray for restoration of the limbs.

Other types of problems caused by a virus that can be dealt with in a similar manner include:

INFLUENZA   SMALL POX
MUMPS   CHICKEN POX
COMMON COLD   MEASLES
RESPIRATORY INFECTION   AIDS
SORE THROATS   RUBELLA
HERPES   GASTROENTERITIS
VARIOUS   CANCERS
WARTS   HEPATITIS

Don't Worry

As you start off, you may find cases that you are still not sure about. In these cases, don't think about yourself and what you are going to say. Think of the people, and that Jesus wants to see them healed.

I, for one, hate to see the devil attacking and winning in peoples' lives and bodies. A righteous anger rises up in me, and I become determined to see that person set free. I have found that as I think about getting the sickness off them, the right words automatically come.

We are all little children, learning more about healing from day to day. God is restoring knowledge to His body, to carry out His will of healing.

None of us has ALL the answers yet.

I remember more than once asking the Holy Spirit to 'MAKE THIS LEG GROW TO THE SAME LENGTH AS THE OTHER', only to find that the other leg grew shorter.

His healing power and knowledge are greater than our sometimes misdirected prayers. He has still, however, ordained this healing to flow through us in spite of our shortcomings.

I have found that if you have a heart and desire to see sickness removed from peoples' lives, then you are moving in line with God's heart of compassion. His grace has sustained me many times.

We know more and are seeing more - different kinds of healings happen this year from those we did last year. We are expecting even greater results next year, as we get more insight into God's word and grow in faith.

I know this - that it is God's will for us to grow into the fulness of His Son, and as we continue to do that, greater things are going to be seen through His saints as a body.

Through perseverance and a love to see the world set free of affliction, you will grow to the greater heights God has for you.

Dr Richard S. Williams
M.B., B.S. Geelong

"Leprosy is caused by an organism akin to that of tuberculosis and particularly attacks the nerves and the skin. This causes loss of function of particular nerves, resulting in loss of sensation in the skin. The anaesthetised skin loses its vitality being insensitive to pain and is not protected if burnt or injured and generally becomes ulcerated and infected leading to loss of the fingers.

I was able to examine many lepers before and after prayer for healing and in every case noted that hands or fingers which were previously insensitive to touch, received an immediate return of sensation after prayer.

What particularly interested me, was seeing a leper who had been prayed for the previous year, still had sensation in his hands and feet and normal skin with no more sores or ulcers - his healing had remained. This return of sensation was greeted with smiles of pleasure on the lepers faces.

Although modern medicine, with the use of drugs can stop the progress of leprosy and by means of operations, pioneered by missionary doctors, can restore function to damaged hands and limbs, it is not able to cause return of nerve function like this. This instant return of sensation in my opinion was a miracle".

154

Chapter 15

GIFTS OF HEALINGS

Our prior recipes for healing have been based absolutely on faith. Preaching the Gospel first, raising a faith expectancy and then either casting a spirit out or laying hands on the person.

Every affliction - leprosy, blindness, cancer, polio - can be healed by faith in Jesus Christ.

"All things are possible to him that believes."

However, we now come to another entirely different way that God can heal. This method is called 'Gifts of Healings' and is listed along with other gifts in 1 Corinthians 12:9.

Many have thought you had to have 'Gifts of Healings' to heal people, but as you well realise from the teaching so far, this is not the case.

I know Christians that have prayed for the sick with no apparent results. The enemy has then flooded them with seeds of doubt. He uses their partial knowledge of Scriptures for healing to confuse them, and rob them of their right to pray for the sick.

Do All Have Gifts of Healings?

This question is asked in 1 Corinthians 12:30: *"Do all have Gifts of Healings?"* In context, the answer to it is...No! Not everyone has "Gifts of Healings" operating.

But as you already realise from our earlier teaching, you don't need Gifts of Healings to see people healed. This is just a different recipe, another way, for the healing power of God to flow.

"My people are destroyed for lack of knowledge..."(Hosea 4:6). For some, their confidence in praying for the sick has been destroyed because of the lack of knowledge in the different ways God heals.

I know some who have prayed with no results and said: "Oh well, I just haven't got "it" (referring to the Gifts of Healings); I'll just wait on God until He reveals what MY ministry really is."

Many just continue to wait...and wait...and WAIT!

You may not have had a gift of healing operating at that time, but the "it" missing may have been the lack of knowledge of the other ways that God can heal.

Praying for healing has to be available for all believers; the Scriptures can't contradict themselves.

"These signs (of healing) shall follow those who believe."

"He who believes on Me the works that I do shall he do also."

Firstly -   Every believer can minister healing by preaching, raising faith and laying on hands.

Secondly -   As the Spirit wills, the believer can be used as an instrument through whom a gift of healing can flow.

What's the Difference?

I can find three basic differences between our recipe for healing in Mark 16 and our Gifts of Healings recipe.

FIRSTLY - As He wills.

The preaching of the Gospel was that ALL who heard,

believed and came to Him were healed. It was based on the faith of the believers. *"...And great multitudes followed Him, and He healed them all."* (Matthew 12:15). *"And the whole multitude sought to touch Him, for power went out from Him and healed them all."(Luke 6:19).* A gift of healing is operated by God sovereignly and only operates as He wills. God will choose the person that He wants to heal by this method, and then select the person through whom this gift will operate.

SECONDLY - The person praying.

Because He is releasing His sovereign gift, it can surpass even the faith of the person praying. This gift has flowed through me on many occasions when my faith was not high enough for the situation. I can remember on one occasion quite a few years ago in India, all the "bad cases" of polio lined up for prayer. After the first twenty and no apparent results, I felt depressed, and the hope of seeing any results began to vanish. The next boy who was bought to me, was carried by his mother. I placed my hands on him just as I had with the others. I heard a grinding kind of sound and then felt his legs move. His mother put him down jubilant, as he was able to walk unaided! It certainly was not my faith - it was a sovereign gift of God, and I was used as the delivery boy!

THIRDLY - The person being prayed for.

We have stressed so far the importance of "believing that you receive and you shall have." In this case however, the power released through the gift surpasses even that of the person being prayed for.

We have an example of this in John 5:1-4, where at the pool of Bethesda, Jesus raises a crippled man.

"In these lay a great multitude of sick people, blind, lame, paralyzed, waiting for the moving of the water. For an angel went down at a certain time into the pool and stirred up the water; then whoever stepped in first, after the stirring of the water, was made well of whatever disease he had." (John 5:3,4).

One person present was a man who had been a cripple for thirty eight years. He could never have been first into the pool, however, as he had no one to help him.

Jesus talked to this man, but he DIDN'T PREACH THE GOSPEL TO HIM. He simply said: "Do you want to be made well?"

No Faith in Jesus

He was unlike all the others who heard the good news about Jesus.

He was unable to cry out like blind Bartimaeus: "Jesus Thou son of David have mercy on me."

He did not have the great faith of the centurion, who said: "But only speak a word and my servant will be healed."

He didn't even reach out in faith like the woman with the issue of blood and say to herself: "If I could but touch the hem of His garment I would be healed."

The man had not heard the Gospel. He had no faith in Jesus. In fact he didn't even know it was Jesus standing before him.

"But the one who was healed did not know who it was..." (verse 13).

He could only conceive of being healed by one method, getting into the pool. Obviously even this was an impossibility to him because his sole answer to Jesus' question was: *"Sir, I have no man to put me into the pool when the water is stirred up; but while I am coming, another steps down before me." (verse 7).*

There was no faith in the man, only despair and disillusionment. What was Jesus' response to the faithless response?

"Rise, take up your bed and walk!"

The man was instantly healed and walked.

How was it possible? A gift of healing had operated, as no receiving faith was required on the part of this man.

We have had other Scriptures that tell us that Jesus healed them "all". However, here Jesus healed only one of the multitude that were in need of help.

I have been in meetings many times where this same principle of "one" healed among hundreds has applied.

Out of a huge crowd only a relatively few, say ten to fifteen, would be healed on a Word of Knowledge and then followed by Gifts of Healing operating.

Many times this happens even before we preach the Gospel.

Why Only One?

We see in John 5 two examples of the Gifts of Healings operating side by side.

Firstly, under the Old Covenant through the pool, and secondly under the New Covenant through Jesus.

We see under the Old Covenant, even though hundreds needed healing, only one would be healed each time as the angels stirred the water.

Jesus walked into the hundreds that needed healing and healed only the one cripple.

After reading through this Scripture a few times, I began to ask the Lord. "Why only one?"

It seemed a little unfair to me at the time, that in other places "all" were healed and yet here under both the Old and New Covenant, only one was healed.

The Lord showed me that He was not unfair, and in fact was being more than fair in dealing with them.

He made a promise in His Covenant that He would heal the sick. *"I Am the Lord that heals you." (Exodus 15:26)*

But nowhere in His Covenant did He promise a pool complete with an angel stirring the water!

Previous generations didn't have the pool, they had to believe and receive healing by faith.

This pool was a gift of healing. It was not something they were entitled to, but a sovereign act of God.

However He showed me that as the "one" was healed, everyone at the pool could have - and should have - been healed at the same time.

They simply had forgotten their Covenant promise.

"Bless the Lord, O my soul, and forget not all His benefits, who forgives all your iniquities who heals all your diseases..." (Psalm 103:2,3)

At any time, even prior to coming to the pool, they could have been all healed by simply believing God's Covenant promise and turning to Him. However the people at that time had a problem.

"For this people's heart is waxed gross, and their ears are dull of hearing, and their eyes they have closed; lest at any

time they should see with their eyes, and hear with their ears, and should understand with their heart, and should be converted, and I should heal them." (Matthew 13:15 K.J.V.).

Because of the hard heart and spiritual blindess of the majority of this "evil and adulterous generation", many were unable to receive in a normal faith manner.

Our Covenant

Our Covenant with Jesus tells us we have benefits as well.

1 Peter 2:24 tells us: *1"Who Himself bore our sins in His own body on the tree, that we, having died to sins, might live for righteousness - by whose stripes you were healed."*

We can also have the benefits of forgiveness and healing as we turn to him in faith and open ourselves up to receive. However, we also live today in an evil and adulterous generation and a majority who, because of their hardened hearts and spiritual blindness, cannot reach out and receive these benefits by faith.

Because of His love for these, He provides a "pool" or gift of healing to demonstrate His reality.

Because of His love for them, He extended the normal boundaries of His agreement and provided them a sign and wonder to show that He was a God capable of keeping His side of the Covenant.

Under the Old Covenant as soon as the "one" was healed, it should have acted as a catalyst to turn them back to God and say: "Lord we are sorry, we did forget all your benefits. Forgive all our iniquities and heal all our diseases."

As a keeper of His own Covenant, He would have been under the obligation of His own Word to heal every one of them.

Healing and Repentance

The Lord went on to show me much more of His wisdom in dealing with the hearts of people. As previously mentioned, the people at that time had become hard hearted, self-righteous and had forgotten God's benefits. That is why Jesus was sent at that time.

As much as God wanted everybody healed, He wanted something far greater.

HE WANTED THEM!

The people around the pool weren't seeking God - they just wanted a healing.

If God had kept stirring the waters until they were all healed, I wonder how many would have turned up next day in the synagogue praising Him.

The majority would have gone back to their previous lifestyles. We see Jesus trying to stop this very thing happening to the crippled man.

After he was healed, Jesus gave him the Gospel, the good news that would keep him in relationship with God and would protect him from further ailments or sicknesses.

"...See, you have been made well. SIN NO MORE, LEST A WORSE THING COME UPON YOU." (John 5:14)

This is what we see today in many of our evangelistic meetings.

We see relatively few healed by gifts, but what effect can that have upon the unsaved person or the backslider?

It demonstrates we do have a powerful God who is showing His reality and ability to keep His Covenant of forgiving their sin and healing their bodies. After seeing the one "healed" they have not only the opportunity of being healed, but coming into a complete relationship with Jesus.

They too can turn to Him IN FAITH and say: "Lord, we didn't realise you provided all these benefits. Forgive us our iniquities and heal this body." God today, under obligation to His own word acts on this pure child like-faith and forgives and heals.

Christians and the Gift

After witnessing the unsaved or other Christians healed through a gift operating, many then decide: "I'm going to receive my healing by a gift."

They start going from evangelist to evangelist, meeting to meeting, "pool to pool", hoping to be the first when the waters of the Holy Spirit stir.

WE DON'T DECIDE IF WE ARE GOING TO RECEIVE BY A GIFT - GOD DOES.

The obvious truth is that not everyone is going to be healed by the "pool" method.

It is only ONE way that God heals.

Hundreds of people would have died sitting around the pool waiting for their opportunity to be "the one".

This could have been avoided obviously if they had not "forgotten all his benefits" and returned to Him in faith.

Many Christians need to re-evaluate their faith and instead of putting their time into running around from meeting to meeting, they need to put the same time into God's word. Establish a heart faith and relationship that will see you not only through your immediate sickness, but give you a basis to receive on future occasions.

Combined Giftings

Quite often two separate gifts can be combined together to see a result. I remember one in a meeting in India, walking up to a crippled man in the front row of the church, grabbing him by the arm and pulling him up and commanding "Get up and walk!" Before I knew it, he was standing and walking.

As soon as it happened, the reality of the situation struck me.

What if he hadn't walked?

He would have ended up flat on his face in front of everyone.

Obviously God had moved above my faith level. Using the Gift of Faith and a Gift of Healing in one combined effort.

Raising the dead

I believe the Gift of Faith and the Gift of the Working of Miracles operates in raising the dead.

It is pretty apparent that you can't preach the Gospel to the person and raise faith.

Obviously God doesn't want every dead person raised, and operates the gift "as He wills". This is an area in which we will see an increase in the coming years. We must be aware God still wants to do it and have an ear to hear, so we can co-operate with His will.

Gifts in you

As we have previously stated, the gifts are another way of healing, and God may choose to operate His healing gifts through you from time to time.

One of the great benefits of course is that it can operate way beyond your normal faith level, and acts as a booster to your ability to believe God.

"Now to Him who is able to do exceeding abundantly above all that we ask or think, according to the power that works in us." (Ephesians 3:20).

We are told to earnestly desire spiritual gifts. The fact that you are reading this book shows an "earnest desire" to heal the afflicted.

Do pray that the Lord would release in you this extra weapon that will help you break through in situations.

When faced with a tough situation, ask the Lord what He wants to do. If you don't sense any leading to operate in a gift, then go back to our first recipe of preaching the Gospel first.

Our experience has been in our crusades, that although Gifts of Healings have flowed, the vast majority have been healed on our first recipe. Let's continue to preach and raise faith because:

ALL THINGS ARE POSSIBLE TO HIM THAT BELIEVES.

Chapter 16

KEEPING YOUR HEALING

We have placed the manifestation of healings into two basic categories. Firstly those who are healed instantly, and secondly those who recover over a period of time.

In a previous chapter we discussed what to do during the recovery period. This chapter covers the problem faced by those who were healed and then tell us: "I've 'lost' my healing!"

Parable Of the Cold

Imagine if you caught a cold, took some medicine, went to bed and within a day or so you were totally healed. You go back to work, and one week later you go down with a cold once again.

Did you "lose" your healing, or did you simply catch another cold? If you were totally healed previously, then obviously you caught another dose.

If you were prayed for and Jesus totally healed you, then you were healed.

However, the devil's job is to kill, steal and destroy and he is desiring to give you another dose of the same sickness, just as in our example of the cold.

Christians, because of ignorance of God's word, give him openings for successful attacks.

Examining how we catch colds can give us some spiritual examples of how to close these openings and avoid further affliction.

One area that will open us up to a cold is a lack of

proper vitamins.

Without a correct diet the amount of Vitamin C, which builds your cold resistance, can be so low that cold after cold can come upon you.

For our spiritual example, the cold obviously relates to the recurring sickness and the Vitamin C is equivalent to your faith resistance level.

Counter Attack

After you receive your healing, the devil begins his counter attack.

He needs first to break through your Vitamin C resistance faith. You will remember from our teaching on recovery that he initially sends the bacteria of fear and doubt.

"Perhaps this healing is just psychosomatic!"

"We'll see if it's still better in the morning!"

"Maybe the doctor's medicine you've been taking has finally done its job!"

"God doesn't love you!"

"You really don't deserve this healing!"

A doubt can begin to rise in your heart.

After suffering a few of these faith destroying attacks, some holes now start to appear in your faith resistance shield.

He fires through and suddenly you feel a small pain in the healed area.

The bacteria continue their second wave of attack.

"You see! It's coming back!"

"You are losing your healing!"

"Jesus doesn't want to heal you!"

Wake up!

No, you are not losing your healing! It's another sickness trying to establish a foothold.

You have two choices. Receive more of it, or repel it.

As soon as the smallest symptom of pain appears, attack it with praise, exactly the same way we taught in the principle of recovery.

"Thank You Jesus that You have healed my body."

"I thank You for the protection of Your Covenant."

"I praise You that by Your stripes I am healed."

Remember Abraham. He "grew strong and was empowered by faith as he gave praise and glory to God". Praising Jesus will raise that empowering faith, your "Vitamin C" resistance level, and will repel and protect you from further attacks.

Perhaps through ignorance you may have allowed the pain to gain a complete foothold, or possibly have received the complaint back in its fulness. You will need to start again and repeat the prayer to remove the spirit or physical impairment once again.

Be prepared the second time to withstand any further attacks with praise and thanksgiving.

The Second Way

You can also catch a cold by disobeying natural principles or laws.

If you went out unprotected on a chilly wet day, and then sat around for hours in your saturated clothes, you create an opening for a cold.

You have broken a natural principle that even your normal body resistance could not override.

God also has spiritual laws that, if disobeyed, can leave us open to further attacks.

After Jesus raised a cripple, recorded in John 5, He gave him some advice, some good news that would keep him free from further attacks of sickness. He told him: "Sin no more lest a worse thing come upon you."

If you continued to break a natural law like persevering to go out unprotected in the rain, you would catch another cold. In fact a worse thing such as influenza or pneumonia could come upon you.

Jesus' Gospel was a Gospel of repentance.

Repentance means to change your direction.

Do it His way now, not your way.

God wants us to obey His rules and principles, not to reduce our freedom, but to benefit us. They ensure our eternal life, but also He knows that they will enable us to live in righteousness, peace and joy in our present lives.

He wants us to obey His laws to keep us free from further attacks of sickness from the enemy.

Unforgiveness

We have found one law that is regularly broken and so causes a hindrance to God's healing power.

The principle is unforgiveness.

Through our teaching we have stressed the importance of Mark 11:24:

"...Whatever things you ask when you pray, believe you receive them and you will have them."

This is our faith Scripture. However, there is a condition under which Mark 11:24 operates, and this is given in the following verses:

"And whenever you stand praying, if you have anything against anyone, forgive them, that your Father in heaven may also forgive your trespasses.

"But if you do not forgive, neither will your Father in heaven forgive your trespasses." (Mark 11:25-26)

Unforgiveness, resentment and bitterness towards others is breaking one of God's rules.

Just as the natural body's resistance could not keep the cold away when the law of wet clothes was broken, our faith cannot override the breaking of this spiritual law.

It can affect us in two ways. Firstly the sickness will not move in the first place. Secondly we may get initial results but the affliction comes back within a short period of time.

Seminar Release

In our seminars we teach the principles in this book, and then those who are taught pray for one another.

Usually we see about 70%-80% healed within a minute or so.

In one of our workshops I noticed, in one area of need, the percentage healed was very low - only about one third of them had received.

I asked the Lord what to do, and He told me to ask how many had been badly hurt emotionally by someone. The majority of those not healed put their hands up.

I told them that by remembering the incident, only one person was really being hurt by it - themselves.

We led them in a prayer forgiving those who had hurt them, and then prayed again for healing.

Immediately, another 40% received healing!

We have since broken this hindrance on a regular basis by using the same prayer.

Prayer Example

"Lord you know all things and you are aware how ...(Name)...has hurt me. However, I realise that by keeping the memory of that incident alive, it doesn't affect them, it only further afflicts me.

"Lord I forgive...(Name)...of all they have done, and I ask that by your Spirit, you minister to my heart and erase the memory and the pain of that incident. I receive that right now and thank You for it, in the Name of Jesus Christ."

Arthritis Defeated

I used to pray for the sick at regular midweek healing services. Quite a few people would come back time after time for the same aches and pains.

I was quite concerned for them, and after questioning a few, found the pain left instantly but returned within a few days.

They were coming to the meeting for their regular spiritual pain killing injection.

I finally realised that unforgiveness was the most common blockage, and was able to release most of them into permanent healing through a forgiveness prayer.

One lady who was in her seventies was suffering from arthritis she told me of her daughter who had hurt her many years previously. I tried to persuade her to forgive that daughter.

"I won't," she said, "you don't know how much she hurt me!"

The pain became worse but she wouldn't let go of that hurt and just continued to come every week for her regular "fix".

Worse pain had come upon her and would continue until she repented and conformed to God's principles.

Your Ministry

If you come across afflicted people who, even after waiting for a reasonable recovery time, or like our old lady are having constant relapses, check to see if unforgiveness is the blockage.

If there is no unforgiveness towards others, place them on a diet of God's Word. We have found it is a lack of faith that is the problem in the majority of cases.

Teach them to praise, and make intercession by speaking in tongues, to raise the resistance level. Also teach them the initial prayer you prayed for them, so they can attack the affliction if it does manage to gain a foothold once again.

My Attacks

At the age of nineteen, I severely damaged my back playing football. My spine was actually bent out of shape into an "S" causing continuous knife-like pain. After an operation and six weeks in hospital I was still left with continuous pain and restricted movement. If I tried to touch my toes I could only just reach past my knees. I wore a brace and used a walking stick.

Some eight years later, I became a Christian and was

prayed for. All the pain left me and I was able to move freely and touch my toes once again.

A year or so later I was playing a game of tennis and suddenly I felt like somebody had hit my back with an iron rod. Pain flooded into my back.

"My back's gone again," was the immediate thought that raced into my mind. I was about to limp off the court. Fortunately at that stage I had been taught on some of the principles of faith.

"If I was healed a year ago ... I am healed. The devil is just putting another attack on me," I reasoned.

"Get off me in Jesus Name," I yelled.

My tennis partner thought I was getting angry with him. I then continued to play tennis. I kept praising God and thanking Him for my healing. It took about 10 minutes for all that pain to go, and I was then able to finish the game with no discomfort.

About twelve years later I was digging in the garden when suddenly I was hit with pain again. It was much worse than the tennis encounter, and when I examined myself my spine was twisted grotesquely once again, the same way it was from the football game in my teens.

My wife, Mary, was upset after I had struggled up the stairs and she saw the shape of my spine. Immediately floods of fears and doubts flowed into my mind.

"Another operation!

Another 6 weeks on my back in hospital!

After that I'll just have to rest up and take things easier."

Suddenly I came to myself. "Don't be a fool!" I said. "You're still a young man who needs plenty of exercise.

It's not God's will to have you acting like an eighty-year-old when you're in your forties."

For that moment I had let fear and doubt erase the memory of God's principles that I had taught others. I was angrier than a hornet and said: "Devil, you are up to your old tricks again."

I prayed immediately and told that sickness to leave. My back was still tender and it felt like I needed some physiotherapy. I went back down to the garden and declared to the Lord that I was believing with every movement and every shovel full of dirt, that it was going to exercise my back into full recovery. Within three days my spine was perfectly straight again and I was healed.

We must realise the devil will come around from time to time, testing you out and trying to find a hole in your faith. That happened when he tested Jesus in the desert.

"Now when the devil had ended every temptation, he departed from Him until an opportune time." (Luke 4:13).

The devil will look for an "opportune time" to put sickness on you. It may be a few minutes after your healing, a few days, months or even years.

The weapons of praise and faith will work for you, if you, remember to use them.

Dr. Allan Cameron
Buderim, Queensland

In the Christian field, we see healing that goes beyond the understanding and explanation of the medical profession. We cannot explain miracles clinically. I have however learnt to expect and believe the promise of healing found in the gospels.

Healings and miracles as occurred in the days of Jesus occur today. As a medical practitioner, I can confirm witnessing such events.

Chapter 17

FURTHER GUIDANCE

Through dissecting the different recipes for healing, we have come up with many basic ingredients for our healing prayers.

When making a cake, a cook will have different ingredients at his disposal - flour, eggs, sugar, etc. Different cakes of course will have different individual recipes, requiring different ingredients each time.

Each time we pray, the complaint can be different, and we will need correct ingredients for that particular disorder. The recipe in each case must come from the Holy Spirit.

You must realise that, although we have given you two basic starter prayers, there is no exact formula for healing. We can see from the example of Jesus that He prayed in a great variety of ways.

In Luke 13, when Jesus used the ingredient of "commanding" to remove the spirit of infirmity from a woman, He combined it with the ingredient of "laying on of hands". *"Woman you are loosed from your infirmity...and He laid His hands on her..." (Luke 13:12,13).*

It would be wonderful, one might think, if we could just produce a book with every formula for healing in it. How easy it would be. A person with no sight would come to us - we would simply open the book and in alphabetical order look under the "B's" "Ah, here it is, 'BLINDNESS'!"

Example: Blind man, John 9:1-7.

Steps: (1) Spit on the ground;
            (2) Make some clay;
            (3) Rub it into the afflicted area;
            (4) Tell patient to go and wash in a pool
                (preferably at Siloam).

Result: Wait a few minutes and your patient is able to
            watch T.V. that afternoon!

Extra Tips:Results seem to be better if done on the
           Sabbath.

Ridiculous, isn't it? Jesus was led by the Spirit to do this miracle this particular way. Another blind man received different treatment. Jesus *"...spit on his eyes and put His hands on him." (Mark 8:23).*

This time Jesus did not spit onto the ground, but directly into his eyes.

Obviously we cannot be tempted into thinking that even recorded Scripture is the only way the Spirit moves.

"And there are also many other things that Jesus did, which if they were written one by one, I suppose that even the world itself could not contain the books that would be written." (John 21:25).

Different Teachings

These different ingredients explain why there has been confusion in the teaching of how to pray for the sick.

I've been to some churches where EVERY prayer for sickness is shouted or commanded. They see SOME results.

Others less inclined to this noisy kind of prayer react

and say: "That's not for us, we'll pray quietly." Again SOME results are seen with the laying on of hands.

Others, again, have relied entirely on Word of Knowledge and Gifts of Healings, and have believed healing only operates when God wants to. They sit back and wait for the moving of the pool. Once, again, SOME results are witnessed.

Can we begin to see that all ways are correct. However if we want to see the fulness of what God wants to do, we must be open to move in every way that God has provided for us and not be limited to one particular doctrine or teaching. Only by using ALL His ways can we move into the realm of seeing "all" healed.

Love - The Key to Guidance

You may now be feeling, with so many different ways God moves, that as a beginner you will be unable to be led.

There are two ways to overcome this:

1. Study

Read the early chapters of this book over and over. Learn every ingredient by heart and also the two basic prayers we have given you. Use these basic prayers and they will give you initial results.

After a few prayer attempts, you will learn to relax a little more and not be so worried about the actual prayer format.

This will make it easier to move on to more Spirit-led prayers.

2. Love

The key to having the Holy Spirit work through you is

not to be thinking: "What am I going to say?"

Who are you thinking about when you do that?

Yourself!

When you think of yourself and your abilities, you WILL become fearful.

You are to think only of that person and the suffering they are going through.

Your love for them and the desire to set them free will release the bondage of fear.

"...Perfect love casts out fear..." (1 John 4:18).

Now, with all the ingredients built into your heart through study, the Holy Spirit will bring these to your remembrance.

"The Helper, the Holy Spirit... He will teach you all things and BRING TO YOUR REMEMBRANCE ALL THINGS THAT I SAID TO YOU." (John 14:26).

With the pure motivation of love towards the person, and now not being worried about yourself, the right words will flow automatically.

Before praying, simply ask the Lord to guide you, and as you do the Spirit-led prayers will flow.

One lady on her first campaign with us in India had learned just the basics of prayer. In only her second night of praying for the sick, she laid hands on a blind boy and he was instantly healed. The people around her became excited and immediately led her to a paraplegic woman seated in a wheel chair.

How would you like to face that challenge as a beginner?

To make things a little more difficult, they informed her that the paraplegic was also dumb.

179

She was taken aback, but felt so sorry for the woman. Suddenly words just came out of her.

She commanded: "You are going to stand up, you are going to walk and you are going to say, 'Praise the Lord'!"

That is exactly what happened. The paraplegic was wonderfully healed and was able to speak.

I know the reality of this story, as the woman who prayed for that cripple was my own mother!

She returned to her hometown in Australia and has since ministered healing to many, many people.

With this attitude, we have found even apparent failures turned into victories.

As Christians learning to move into this new dimension of healing, there will be times we don't attain to our full potential in doing the works that Jesus did.

We can pray, and find the sickness has not gone. This happened to me many times in my days as a younger Christian and still does today. I have by no means reached the fullest potential that Jesus has for me.

However, even in these times I noted one thing. The people I prayed for saw that I earnestly cared for them and that I simply wanted to help them. My prayer and the laying on of my hands was an expression of that compassion. I have seen tough fully grown men weep as I prayed, simply because somebody finally showed them the love of Jesus.

In these seeming failures of healing they were drawn by that compassion and many of them recovered later anyway.

Isn't it wonderful to know that with a correct attitude of

wanting to help others, we can do nothing else but demonstrate His heart for a hurting world?

Who Do I Pray For?

We dealt with the guidance needed in the individual prayer, but we need guidance also in who we pray for.

We obviously have two basic groups involved here:

1. Christians; and
2. Non Christians.

Let's first of all discuss the various groupings in Christian circles and then others.

Family and Body of Christ

We can pray in total confidence for our family and other members of the Body of Christ. God has already given His word that: *"By whose stripes you were healed." (1 Peter 2:24)*. This is for all believers. Many of us in the Body have not appropriated this promise.

"My people are destroyed through lack of knowledge." (Hosea 4:6). But through your new-found knowledge and authority, you can help break through the barriers, to see God's Word fulfilled in their lives. The absence of sickness in a Christian family should be a witness and a talking point to other unsaved families. Your family should be a "centre of healing" for your district. Wouldn't it be wonderful to see sick people sitting in your lounge instead of at the doctor's waiting room? What a wonderful witness!

"My baby is sick," one might say.

"Well, just go and see Mrs Smith, up the road; she is a Christian and will pray for you," her neighbour would answer.

Preach to Christians?

However many times when we come across Christians, we can assume they already have faith. I have had many occasions when we have had to battle with unbelief. They may never have had any teaching previously, or even worse, wrong teaching.

Don't ever assume Christians know the entire Gospel, or that they believe it.

It is your job with both Scripture and personal experiences of yourself and others to remove all unbelief and doubt. To get them to open their heart and expect to receive.

Praying for Myself?

Yes, you can pray for yourself. It is the same principle as a doctor giving himself a needle and injecting a vaccine which will heal him.

By laying hands on yourself, you can inject that Holy Spirit power into the afflicted part of your body.
Some Christians seem to have difficulty in believing in this area.

Our experience has been that some beginners seem to have much more faith to pray for others than for themselves. In that case, get another person to pray with you and believe with them that God's power goes into you.

Use the principle in Matthew 18:19: *"... If two of you agree on earth concerning anything that they ask, it will be done for them by My Father in heaven."*

Praying for Children

Obviously, Jesus wants to heal children. He said in

Mark 10:14: *"Let the little children come to Me, and do not forbid them..."*

Our experience has been that if the child is too young to understand the Gospel and believe for itself, then you need to work through their parents and their faith. A parent is the covering for the child.

"For the unbelieving husband is sanctified by the wife, and the unbelieving wife is sanctified by the husband; otherwise your children would be unclean, but now they are holy." (1 Corinthians 7:14).

You must preach the Gospel to the parents, and if they open up and give permission, then you pray for the children.

However, an unbelieving parent can be leaving a child open to be attacked again.

Many times we have found in India after praying for, say, deaf and dumb children of Hindu parents, they are instantly healed. They go back to an environment where the parents are praying to the spirits of their gods. The child, being unprotected, can be attacked by the deaf and dumb spirits again. Fortunately this has been a great witness in many cases with the parent. They turn back to Jesus, realising His power is the only thing that will protect their homes and children on a permanent basis.

Can Non—Christians Receive Healing Before Salvation?

The question is often asked, can an unsaved person receive the promise of healing!

In the book of Luke, ten lepers cried out for healing. One of these was a foreigner and wouldn't have been under the Covenant. Jesus simply said: *"Go, show yourselves to the priests." (Luke 17:14)* As they went, they were cleansed.

Note, Jesus didn't say to them: "If you men go to church, learn fifty Scriptures, stop smoking and drinking and be good for 6 months, then I'll heal you."

No! He asked nothing of them except to act in faith. What was the end result?

Only one came back and fell at His feet, signifying his recognition of the Lordship of Jesus.

He gave the "sign" of His Lordship to all ten. Nine took the sign of healing. One came back to take eternal life as well.

Remember our story with the air hostess - she was healed first and received Christ later.

My Early Mistake

I found in my initial enthusiastic witnessing I lost many people. I used to try to forcefeed the Gospel of eternal life down their throats.

Many people today, because of "gross darkness", have initially great difficulty in believing in God. They spat my Gospel medicine out.

After quite a few knockbacks, I found that these same people were quite often willing to allow me to pray for physical healing.

After that success, they could see the reality of God and then were willing to take a mouthful of eternal life.

Yes, we obviously can pray for the unsaved and they

can receive their healing. However, unless they give their lives to Jesus, they do not come under the covering and protection that He offers.

If they continue without Jesus, they can open themselves up to further attacks of sickness.

Remember what Jesus said to the cripple that He healed: *"Sin no more, lest a worse thing come upon you."*

Which Unsaved Do I Pray For ?

Obviously, with the newfound knowledge and boldness, many may want to race out and lay hands on every unsaved person and change the world overnight.

Personally, I'd rather see the church full of 'GO-ers' rather than "WHOA-ers". Jesus' disciples are goers, for He has already commanded us, "GO YE"! At least, when you are moving, God can steer you and begin to change your direction as required.

He is our rudder, but He cannot direct a ship that is continually moored at the docks. If we just sit, waiting for something to happen, it usually doesn't.

For the goers, however, here are some words of advice that may prevent you from running out of breath in your race to change the world. When I was a younger "GOER", I perpetually said to the Lord after some of my failures: "I really believed for him, Lord; he should have been healed." Or: "Why didn't he get healed Lord?" I was almost angry at God.

My faith teaching had declared to me that "I" was in command, "I" was the one with power and authority.

" 'I' can do all things through Christ who strengthens me."

(Philippians 4:13).

God has a plan for each of us to be used in seeing the "good news" come to fruition in others' lives. The Kingdom of God is not won by man deciding what is best and attempting to persuade God to do it. The Kingdom is won by God deciding what is desirable, and guiding His people into obeying it. This obedience will ensure that we pray in line with God's will, and it will assure us of results.

How then do I get direction for the unsaved?

Firstly, after all this teaching, our prayers for guidance change. We no longer pray:

"What is my ministry?"

"Am I to heal?"

"Will You use me?"

That kind of prayer IS FINISHED !

We no longer need guidance in what our ministry is. The only question we need to ask is:

"WHICH PERSON?"

As Jesus went about, His steps were not haphazard. He knew where the Holy Spirit wished to minister, and followed that leading. Each person who approached Him was brought across His path by God. We need to start realising this ourselves. The majority of us cannot be out knocking on doors, preaching on street corners or conducting healing crusades. Every day, however, opportunities are crossing our paths.

In our morning prayers we need to ask the Lord to lead us, or have people led to us, who are in need. The Lord knows those who are open to hear. It may be while you do the shopping, at your work, or in your recreation. After prayer you can relax in the knowledge that God will bring someone across your path.

"Trust in the Lord with all your heart, and lean not on your own understanding; in all your ways acknowledge Him, and He shall direct your paths." (Proverbs 3:5-6).

Do you believe that it is God's will for everyone in your town to hear the Gospel with signs following?

Do you believe He will draw the unsaved to those who are willing to preach and heal? A big "YES" to both questions. THE HARVEST IS PLENTIFUL BUT THE LABOURERS ARE FEW!

I believe God is continually bringing opportunities to us every day of the week. Yet we have rarely realised it, and so have not capitalized on it. We believe that you can relax, knowing that God will draw people across your path.

Asking For The Gospel

People talking to you will often talk about their problems. When they say: "I've got a bad back," don't give your previous answer of: "Well, have you been to see a doctor?"

Tell them you know a cure for it. When they ask for the answer, they have just given you an open invitation to preach the Gospel.

Oblige them with testimonies and stories, and then say: "We can pray right now, would you like me to do that?"

You will be surprised at the results and the openness of the unsaved after divine healing has been explained to them.

Another Blockage

In some undeveloped countries the people in ignorance have gone to witch doctors or sought black magic for healing.

These men quite often pray over charms, necklets and other items asking the aid of evil spirits.

The charms are then hung around the neck, arms legs or stomach of the person.

Praying for such cases met with little success and we asked them to remove them and look only to Jesus Christ.

As soon as they threw them away, we prayed again and met with instant success.

We have witnessed this happening time and time again.

Although you may feel this may only apply to some third world nations, there is an increase in western nations of those practising occult healing. Their power source is the devil and his demonic forces.

In ignorance some people have gone to these, and after failure, have then sought divine healing.

Praying for these usually gives no result or at best temporary healing. A simple renouncement of such methods and opening themselves up to Jesus only will break through the "blockage."

Suggested Prayer

"Lord Jesus, I acknowledge You right now as the one and only true Healer. Please forgive my ignorance. I renounce.................(blackmagic, spiritism, or whatever) and look only to You for my healing."

Chapter 18

FAITH AND DOCTORS

God has on countless occasions worked through dedicated doctors. Prayer has been answered as patients pulled through impossible operations and others have recovered at a "miraculous" rate.

Doctors have been, and will continue to be a blessing to a hurting world. Many of us who are preaching divine healing possibly would not be here today if it hadn't been for medical science.

However, God is restoring wonderful and higher truths for us today. He is wanting us to advance to a higher technology for healing...His spiritual technology.

It is not always easy to get people to change to newer and more efficient methods.

As an example, if I gave you the choice of going from Hong Kong to Los Angeles by aeroplane or by boat, most of us would choose to fly.

It is much easier, quicker and a lot more comfortable to go by plane.

God is today giving us an alternative for our healing. For instance, if you have a tumour you may choose to have an operation. If you are a diabetic you may receive insulin. God is making His alternative of divine healing available and obviously the higher truth is much easier and a lot more comfortable.

It is not always possible for some to jump onto this new method immediately.

I am sure that when planes first crossed the Pacific

there would have been many who would not have had the faith necessary to take such a trip.

Eventually, after hearing first hand stories from others who enjoyed the advantages, and then perhaps taking a few short trips themselves, their confidence grew. Finally they had the faith to step out and fly great distances.

Only a relatively few people today seem to be able to fly great distances instantly with divine healing. We who are praying must understand that in many cases we can't go beyond the persons own faith level.

You cannot impose your faith level on that person. Remember our example of twenty-five-fold, fifty-fold and one-hundred-fold faith.

Operations

The majority of people can take small faith flights and believe God for many smaller ailments. If they are immediately faced with a major decision such as an operation or totally cutting out medication, most cannot make the large jump in faith.

If for example it is an operation for a tumour, ask the person what they can believe God for. They may say: "I can believe God for a perfect operation, little pain after and for the incision to be healed in half the normal time."

Agree with that, and pray. This will be like a short faith trip and after this initial prayer success, their faith will grow and they will be able to believe Jesus for bigger and better things next time.

Medication

I have had others who are on constant medication, ask

after prayer: "Should I throw my pills away?"

The very fact they are asking is an indication that they are not ready to take such a long distance flight.

Again we ask the person what they can believe God for. They may say: "I believe He can heal me over the next ten weeks."

If so, they can believe God can improve their condition by 10% each week, and they adjust their intake of medication in line with the rate that God is healing them.

This is a personal decision. Only they can work at their faith level and only they can determine it. The rate of taking medication is their decision and should be done in co-operation with their doctor.

This way he can monitor their progress, and also gain faith himself as a bonus!

Working in faith and in co-operation with their medical practitioner in different areas can be the first steps to greater and greater faith and healing.

We are all learning to take bigger and greater faith flights, all reaching out to achieve the highest level of faith God wants for us. Christian doctors are growing with us, learning step by step to believe for bigger and greater things every year.

I look forward to the day when both doctors and patients can get out of the boat of medicine and operations and soar with total faith in divine healing.

Your Faith and Doctors

There may be times when you release faith, wait for a reasonable recovery time, and still see no manifestation of healing.

We don't know all the answers. Sometimes it may be lack of faith on our part and other times lack of faith on theirs.

After we have done our best for Jesus, I have no problem if the person wants to go back to the doctor.

If you can't go by plane, then at least go by boat. It's obviously much better than no trip at all!

All of us are still growing into the fulness of faith that Jesus requires of us. I don't know anyone yet who has reached the level of, "the works that I do shall you do also". However this is still my goal, and it should be yours as well.

Each failure acts as a catalyst to make me seek the Lord even further. Each disappointment makes me more determined to build my faith and succeed the next time.

Each year I learn more things and find new ingredients to help set others free. Each year my faith expands and I meet with more successes.

This book is an expansion of my first book on healing. I began teaching the principles and ingredients in 1983. The rewrite was neccessary because of the many extra things I have learnt.

I am trusting in a few short years I will release another rewrite with even more keys.

Medical science is continually experimenting in new areas and discovering further answers to healing.

We are all doctors of the Spirit realm, breaking into new fields as we continue to seek God for revelation on His ways.

Don't be disheartened by failure. Be encouraged by the successes.

Building Yourself Up

There are two things you can do to ensure your continued growing faith and knowledge in this realm.

Firstly, read this book over and over until the principles are part of you.

Always remember ONE MISSING INGREDIENT CAN CAUSE A FAILURE OR FLOP.

A doctor who is praying for the sick told us he had been through our material twelve times and was now recommencing a further study.

Secondly, get other books on the subject. Other writers will give you insights that we have not yet discovered.

Continue practising and learning and slowly, step by step, you will climb up the grades of faith and the numbers healed will increase.

Be like Paul, who said: *"Brethren I do not count myself to have apprehended; but the one thing I do, forgetting those things which are behind and reaching forward to those things which are ahead..." (Philippians 3:13).*

Let's forget the failures and reach forward to greater triumphs as we go on from faith to faith and glory to glory into His image and works.

Dr. Colin H. Walker
Cairns, Queensland

After attending a seminar on divine healing, I began to apply the principles of praying for the sick myself and can now confirm they work.

One of the most notable was a little girl who was suffering from deafness from birth. Normal medical treatment could not help her, after praying she was set free.

Chapter 19

READY FOR ACTION

In Judges, chapter 7, Gideon's army is a very good example of the army Jesus is going to raise in these end times. The different levels of soldiers correspond with many aspects of our Christian walk including healing! A battle was looming and God wanted only top-line fighters. He first asked for all those who were afraid to fight to go back home.

Even today we have a similar problem. There are those soldiers who, through fear, will not move into this exciting realm of warfare and miracles which is awaiting us. Obviously, reading this book, you are one who wishes to go into battle. Let's trust that you can pass the next test God has for you.

Gideon then made his final selection based on the particular way that they drank from the water. The ones who lifted up the water to their mouths with their hands were the only ones allowed to fight in the battle.

Why this strange selection?

Gideon's soldiers were on occupied enemy territory, just as God's army is today. The ones who used their hand as a cup were able to look about and keep alert.

Even in the time required to fill a basic need in their lives, they were on the lookout for the enemy.

The rest of the soldiers went to their knees to drink. They were not worried about the enemy, they were interested only in fulfilling their own needs.

We must be awake at all times, looking for the enemy

and a chance to break his bondage over people's lives.

I wonder how many times we miss opportunities to witness or pray because we are too interested in satisfying our own physical needs. Even when we are eating our lunches, opportunities can open themsleves to present the Gospel in a pleasant atmosphere.

Many times, "I'm too tired" or "I can't be bothered" can see opportunities for people to be healed go begging. In missing these we forgo seeing the joy of other people's lives changed, and the excitement of God working through us.

Sleepy Stuart

Once, while travelling on a bus between preaching engagements, I was really looking forward to having a good sleep during the five hour journey. I had a heavy schedule, and was trusting that I would get a seat beside a person who was not talkative. When I took my place, an elderly woman was already in her seat staring out of the window. I can't recall her name now, but for the sake of the story I'll call her Florence. "Good", I thought to myself. "Just a quiet, sweet old lady, who won't bother me. I'll get plenty of rest."

I put a book I was reading in the open pocket in front of me, relaxed, and closed my eyes. Within a few minutes I was startled by a sharp voice in my ear. "I can see that!" Florence yelled. My whole body came to attention and I spun around to face her eyeball to eyeball. "I can see that," she called again. I must have looked totally puzzled. "That book," she said, pointing to the pocket.

"Good," I said, and nodded my head. "What have we

got here?" I thought to myself, pretending to immediately fall asleep.

A few quiet minutes went by. "It's a Christian book isn't it?" Her deafening voice shattered my tranquility once again. "Yes," I said quite promptly, closing my eyes. Inside, my mind was saying: "I wish she'd be quiet." On her third yell I was completely awake.

"I know about Christianity!"

"Do you?" I said. "Where did you learn that?"

"I beg your pardon," she called again, lifting one hand to her ear. We were already the centre of attention in the bus, but even more so when I screamed back: "Where did you learn that?"

"I was brought up in a Baptist Church as a young girl," she continued in her high tone.

After a few minutes of "high level" conversation, it finally got through to me that she "may have" a hearing defect and "maybe" the Lord wanted to do something about it.

"Have you got a problem with your ears?" I called.

Everyone in the bus was already saying in their minds: "Of course she has, you dummy!"

"I beg your pardon," she called back, placing her hand to her ear once again. My assertion obviously now correct, I told her the good news. In a loud voice I told her that Jesus could heal her if she would allow me to pray for her.

Before I had a chance to pray, a miracle happened. All the necks of the people in the bus grew at least two inches, as they stretched around to get a good look at us. I felt like taking up a collection!

I held Florence's hand and we prayed. Immediately she received a miracle of total healing! There we were, our heads together, Florence with tears of joy flowing down her cheeks. What a sight!

When she disembarked she called out: "Goodbye, I'll never forget you."

I'm sure none of the other passengers would either, because throughout the rest of the trip the people, using their new extended necks, kept looking around to get another look at me.

I could have missed the happiness of that opportunity if Florence had not created the fuss. I trust in God that I keep alert and don't miss any more.

Rivers of Life

There are some Scriptures that have given me wrong concepts. Perhaps, like me, you may have also been hindered and need to be released.

I used to, as a young Christian, read Scriptures like *"He who believes in Me...out of his heart will flow rivers of living water." (John 7:38).*

I would pray: "Lord, I really want that. I sincerely desire the rivers of living water to flow." I was never too sure what I was praying for. I guessed it was some spiritual peak you attained after many years of holiness.

I also read Scriptures like: *"You are the light of the world..." (Matthew 5:14).* I ended up with some very weird concepts. I saw myself developing into a shining light with pure, crystal clear water flowing out from me. Like some glowing statue in a pond with a fountain of water gushing out from my mouth and people being drawn to my light like moths.

Although this example is obviously exaggerated, there are some Christians who feel their witness is to just stand like a light and somehow people will be drawn to their brightness.

What are these rivers of life? *"But this He spoke concerning the Spirit, whom those believing in Him would receive..." (John 7:39)*.

The ministry of the Holy Spirit is to flow through every believer.

Remember we learnt in Luke 4:18:

As we preach the Gospel...a river of life flows out from our mouth. As we open blind eyes...a river of life flows from inside us, along our arms and into the person. As we heal the broken hearted...a river of life flows and touches that hurt. As we set free those who are oppressed...a river of life flows out driving demonic forces away. This is not a "passive statue" concept of the Christian. It is talking of believers who hear the command of Mark 16 to preach, heal, cast out demons - and obey it!

Those who release this kind of ministry will, just as Jesus did, draw people and be the example and light that He always has wanted us to be.

Contagious Goodness

I was meditating on the Scripture of Acts 10:38 where it tells how Jesus, full of the Holy Spirit, *"went about doing good and healing all..."*

Whenever Jesus touched, or came in contact with anyone, He spread healing help and goodness to them. He could do nothing else, because He was full of compassion and wholesomeness.

The Lord said to me: "JESUS WAS CONTAGIOUS GOODNESS!"

I began to grasp the truth. If people were open to Him, they would "catch" what He was spreading. The Lord went on to tell me: "The works that Jesus did, you will do also. YOU ARE CONTAGIOUS GOODNESS!"

The reality of this didn't quite sink in until a crusade in the Indian city of Vijayawada a few months later.

I was preaching and holding onto a leper's hand and suddenly the words once again flowed into my mind: "You are contagious goodness".

Immediately, I grasped what the Lord was saying, I turned to the crowd and said: "Each one of you would be afraid to touch this leper. You would be scared of catching what he has got. Men of God do not have to be afraid of leprosy. Leprosy is afraid of us!"

"I'm not going to catch what he's got. He's going to catch what I've got!"

For about eight years, "contagious badness" had been flowing through this man. However, in a few short seconds, the "contagious goodness" flowed in. He "caught" the healing and was set free.

Contagious Christians

I was listening to an advertisement for fly spray and squirmed as I heard all the vivid details of how filthy a fly is.

It contaminates and pollutes, spreading disease on everything it touches. It was a perfect example of CONTAGIOUS BADNESS.

This is one method which the devil uses to kill, steal and destroy among mankind.

God has a method today of giving life and life more abundantly. Today we have been chosen and empowered to spread healing and goodness to all the earth. Every time you come in contact with people and touch them, you leave restoration and wholeness in your wake.

A fly can't help but spread disease on everything it touches. It is full of contamination. That is its nature.

You have a new nature inside you. Everytime you speak God's word, every time you lay hands on people, you are contagious. You can't help but release goodness and healing on to others because that is what is in you.

In the past you may have had fears of catching sickness and disease from others. We now must realise that when we come in contact with sickness, there is nothing to fear. Just the same as with the leper I prayed for, you are not going to catch something from them. They are going to catch something from you:

YOU ARE CONTAGIOUS GOODNESS!

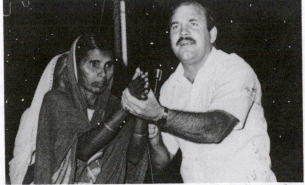

This woman, a leprosy sufferer "caught" divine healing.

— NOTES —

— NOTES —

ORDER FORM

Further copies of this book and others written by Stuart Gramenz are available. Simply fill out the order form below.

	1 — 2 Copies	3 — 5 Copies	10 or More
How to Heal the Sick	$9.90 (each)	$7.90 (each)	$5.90 (each)
How to be Bold as a Lion	$5.95	$4.80	$3.60
Who are Gods Guerrillas	$8.95	$7.20	$5.40

* Prices are quoted in Australian Dollars
* Orders placed in New Zealand please add 10%
* Postage and Handling please add 10% within Australia and New Zealand
* Other Countries please add 20% for Postage and Handling

— —

	No. of Copies	Price	Total
How to Heal the Sick		$	$
How to be Bold as a Lion		$	$
Who are Gods Guerrillas		$	$
Please send to		Sub Total	$
Name...............................		NZ add 10%	$
Address ....Code.......		Postage either 10% or 20%	$
Please find enclosed my cheque for the total amount of			$

NEW ZEALAND	AUSTRALIA
International Outreach	International Outreach
P.O. Box 17-051	P.O. Box 64
GREENLANE	NEWSTEAD
AUCKLAND 5	QUEENSLAND 4007